ScriptWorks 20/20

20 Short Plays *from* 20 Years *of* Out of Ink

© 2018 ScriptWorks

These plays are protected by copyright law. It is illegal to print, transcribe, or otherwise duplicate any play in this publication. The plays are fully protected under the copyright laws of the United States of America and all countries with which the United States has reciprocal copyright relations.

All rights to these plays are strictly reserved, including, without limitation, professional and amateur stage performance rights; motion picture, recitation, lecturing, public reading, radio broadcasting, television, video, and sound recording rights; rights to all other mechanical or electronic production now known or yet to be invented, such as CD-ROM, CD-I, DVD, photocopying, and information storage and retrieval systems; and the rights of translation into non-English languages.

Amateur and stock performance rights to these plays are controlled by their authors. Inquiries concerning all rights should be addressed to the authors directly or via ScriptWorks, www.scriptworks.org.

ScriptWorks is funded and supported in part by a grant from the Texas Commission on the Arts and the City of Austin through the Cultural Arts Division believing an investment in the Arts is an investment in Austin's future. Visit Austin at NowPlayingAustin.com.

Published by ScriptWorks
PO Box 9787
Austin, Texas 78766-9787

Cover and book design by Gordon Haber of Dutch Kills Press.

ISBN-13: 978-1-7322924-0-6

ScriptWorks is dedicated to the living memory of our co-founder David Mark Cohen.

Table of Contents

Introduction i
About ScriptWorks.. ii
OUT OF INK 1999: Biblical Proportions 1
STAY AT HOME, DAD... 2
OUT OF INK 2000: Speaking in Tongues.................... 12
SQUARE PEGS... 14
OUT OF INK 2001: Boot Arias 25
HAZARD... 27
OUT OF INK 2002: Liquid Princesses........................... 39
THE LAST TIME COOPER TOOK MIDGE FISHING 41
OUT OF INK 2003: Sitting Room Only 48
THE CHAIR... 50
OUT OF INK 2004: Of Superheroes and Seductions.... 58
KRYPTONITE... 60
OUT OF INK 2005: Talk Doesn't Cook Rice 72
FAMILY PLANNING 74
OUT OF INK 2006: Cricket Radio 86
WAITING IS NOT MERELY EMPTY HOPING 87
OUT OF INK 2007: Hybrid 94
AMERICAN WOMEN AND THEIR HATCHETS............ 96
OUT OF INK 2008: Key Changes 103
FOR THE FOURTEENTH TIME 105
OUT OF INK 2009: Time Steps................................... 116
COWBOY FANTASIA 118

OUT OF INK 2010: The Trunk Show	127
WHAT HAVE YOU GOT TO LOSE?	129
OUT OF INK 2011: Forgetting Finnegan	136
JOYCE, OR THE UNKNOWING	138
OUT OF INK 2012: Sound Off	145
THE NORTH START TRANSGALACTIC INCIDENT	147
OUT OF INK 2013: Snapshots	158
PLAYDATE	160
OUT OF INK 2014: The Empty Set	174
IT'S TIME	176
OUT OF INK 2015: Random Acts of Magic	189
THE DISAPPEARING ROSE TRICK	191
OUT OF INK 2016: Carry On	204
WATCH	206
OUT OF INK 2017: Object Lessons	217
SMILEY	219
OUT OF INK 2018: Lost & Found	230
BIG BRAD WOLF	232

Introduction

The twenty plays in this volume represent a small fraction of the 500-plus plays written over twenty years of Weekend Flings. Inspired by Paula Vogel's "Bake-offs" and the belief that constraint can arouse creativity, the "Fling" inspires ScriptWorks members to write ten-minute plays over 48 hours using three contributed ingredients (aka rules or elements). Out of Ink is the companion program to the Weekend Fling, where we produce eight to ten of those plays.

Over the last twenty years, ingredients have been provided by local Austin artists as well as luminaries of the new play and theatrical world: Naomi Iizuka, Steven Dietz, Caridad Svich, Todd London, Michael John Garces, Sherry Kramer, Lisa D'Amour, and Liz Engelman, to name a few. They gave our writers the opportunity to wrangle with mysterious liquids, revelatory smells, talking objects, various dances, and all kinds of wrinkles in time. One of the joys of attending Out of Ink is seeing how each writer applies their unique slant to the ingredients. Hopefully, readers will be equally delighted in seeing that originality multiplied across twenty years of ingredients and plays.

We owe a debt of gratitude to all those who contributed ingredients and who have served on Out of Ink selection committees, especially Debbie Lynn Carriger, C. M. Gill, and Patti Neff-Tiven, who helped select the plays included in this book. Special thanks, as well, to Christopher Krejci, who provided vital assistance with copy-editing and proofreading.

Christina J. Moore
Co-Founder and Executive Artistic Director

About ScriptWorks

ScriptWorks exists to support dramatic writers by providing opportunities at all stages in the writing process — from inception through production. ScriptWorks supports the whole writer, not just isolated projects, and dedicates itself to career advancement as well as artistic growth. Our programs encourage members to engage in the **creation, development** and **production** of their plays and provide playwrights the resources to **network** and promote their plays both locally and nationally.

Founded in 1997 as Austin Script Works, the organization is driven by dramatic artists with a commitment to the written word as the integral point of creation. Individual members represent some of the finest regional dramatic writers garnering both local and national recognition from organizations such as: The National Endowment for the Arts, the Kennedy Center Fund for New American Plays, the Austin Critics' Table, the B. Iden Payne Awards, The William Inge Theatre Festival, The Playwright's Center of Minneapolis, the International Hemingway Festival, The Humana Festival, and the Yale Drama Series Prize. Members come from Austin, San Antonio and Dallas/Ft. Worth as well as far-flung cities like New York, Chicago and San Francisco.

OUT OF INK 1999: Biblical Proportions

Ingredients:

1. Use a Bible in a surprising way.
2. Have a revelation involving a smell.
3. Contain no adjectives.

The ingredients were contributed by Vicky Boone (then Artistic Director of Frontera@Hyde Park Productions), Robert Faires, Arts Editor for the Austin Chronicle, and playwright, Sherry Kramer.

The original production ran March 24-28, 1999 at The Public Domain Theater, 807 Congress Ave. in Austin with the following company:

Playwrights: Tim Bauer, Ron Berry, Vicki Caroline Cheatwood, Amparo Garcia, David Gunderson, Clay Nicols, P. Paullette MacDougal, John Walch, Cyndi Williams

Directors: Jim Fritzler, Cathy Hartenstein, Christina J. Moore, Katie Pearl

Performers: Michael Arthur, Mick D'Arcy, Lana Dieterich, Topher Glenn, Mark Greene, Jessica Hedrick, Derek Mudd, Douglas Taylor, and Lara Toner

Designers: Chase Staggs (sets), Kingsley Eliot Haynes (lighting)

Production Staff:
Stage Manager: Jennifer Rogers

ScriptWorks Staff (then Austin Script Works):
Co-Artistic Directors: Clay Nichols, John Walch
Executive Director: Emily Cicchini
Producing Director: Christina J. Moore

STAY AT HOME, DAD
Clay Nichols
© 1999

CHARACTERS

SPEAKER, *50's, hired gun, oozes "charisma"*
DAD, *thirty-something, schlub*
SUIT LADY, *50's, Prada shoes*
TANK-TOP, *20's, oh lord*

SETTINGS

A conference room in Austin, Texas.
A suburban kitchen and driveway.
Outside a Starbucks coffeehouse.

SET

A podium, stage left, equipped with a mic. Several chairs. A tape player down center.

In the dark we hear a tape-player being turned on. Lights up. The SPEAKER approaches the podium. He wears a suit and tie and oozes confidence. He removes cards from his jacket. Gestures to a friend in the audience.

SPEAKER: Bill.

He places his cards on the podium. A spotlight isolates him. He gathers himself for a moment, perhaps clears his throat. Leans into the mic.

SPEAKER: Penis. You titter. I say penis, you titter. Penis. Why do you think that is? Why today, here in Austin, Texas do people laugh when I say penis? Has manhood become a joke here? Clients told me, "you're just wasting time, Thor, manhood is a goner in Austin." But I said, no. I'm going to Austin. Manhood is not dead in Austin. They just don't recognize the opposition. They don't know the face of anti-manhood. So I came. To show you that face.

The SPEAKER clicks his remote and a slide appears. It's one of those Anne Geddes photos of a baby dressed as a daisy.

SPEAKER: Look at this picture and tremble, brothers. (*Click. Another baby slide.*) Hold tight to your manhood and be afraid. (*Click. Another cutie.*) Because if this doesn't frighten you, if this doesn't scare you right to the core of your genitalia...this could happen to your maleness. (*Click. A slide of DAD holding a swaddled infant, beaming like a moron. Lights rise slowly on DAD and infant onstage in the same pose.*) Meet Mr. Mom. Stay-at-home-dad. Pseudo-Male of the 90s. All around him values crumble. Traditions collapse. Manhood shrivels. Which leads me to the question...(*The SPEAKER produces a pointer. Indicates DAD's crotch.*) Penis? Roll tape please. (*DAD comes to life pacing, jiggling the baby. The baby wails unceasingly.*) A client of mine. I wonder sometimes if I need do anything at the seminar but play this tape. I mourn whenever I see it.

Keeping the baby constantly in motion on his shoulder, DAD tries to open a can of formula, pour it into a bottle, and attach a nipple to the bottle. The baby wails. DAD mutters to himself, "Okay, here we go, there we are" etc. He drops the nipple. Ponders this. Does a limbo to pick it up. Wipes it off on his pants.

DAD: Minerals.

> *Click. The slide disappears. DAD feeds the baby. The wail stops.*

SPEAKER: What do you remember of your father? The suits he wore? The briefcase? The scent of the world on his lapels? For me it was the voice.

> *DAD has finished the feeding and is now burping the baby.*

SPEAKER: The depth. Weight. A voice mellowed by whiskeys on the rocks and Chesterfields. The voice of a man.

DAD: (*falsetto, delighted*) Is it a pooky-wooky? I think it's a pooky-wooky. Yes it is a pooky-wooky.

SPEAKER: Like the Castrato of old, no?

DAD: Say, I'm a piggle. Say, I'm just a piggle-wiggler.

SPEAKER: Did Teddy Roosevelt talk this way?

DAD: Booga-booga.

SPEAKER: MacArthur? Alexander the Great? Roger Staubach?

DAD: Shooter-pooter. Are you a shooter-pooter?

SPEAKER: No.

> *Lights shift. DAD exits with the baby.*

SPEAKER: No, and we, today, men, here in Austin, must retain our voices! We must retain the properties that once belonged to the manhood of our fathers! The voice that belonged to our fathers and to their fathers reaching back man to man to the beginning of time. Properties essential to manhood. Voice, one, yes. Voice. But also command! Also command. Roll tape.

> *DAD enters pushing a stroller. He carries a Starbucks cup.*

SPEAKER: Oh, hold it here for a moment. (*DAD freezes. SPEAKER produces the pointer. Indicates the cup.*) Latté. Okay. Roll it.

> *DAD parks the stroller and sits. Sips his latté.*

SPEAKER: Now, I'm no cave man, although the ancestors have much to teach us. I'm no Neanderthal with his club, despite what my critics may say. I simply mean to say someone...Someone...must have Command.

> *The SUIT LADY almost rushes past. She stops, shoves her phone into her purse and ogles the stroller.*

SUIT LADY: Oh, look at you. Look at you. (*to DAD*) Boy?

DAD: Yeah.

SUIT LADY: Fourteen weeks?

DAD: Uh, actually, I think...Let's see...he was born...(*calculating*) Fourteen weeks... exactly.

SUIT LADY: Aren't you a cutie. Yes, you are a cutie. (*She puts her hand into the stroller.*) Oh, my goodness, my feet are freezing. Say, my feet are freezing, dad. Don't you have some socks, Dad?

DAD:	Uh, well, earlier…
SUIT LADY:	And a hat. Can you say, I need a hat, daddy? Say, babies get chilly in this weather, dad.
DAD:	Hats, though…he…
SUIT LADY:	Say, babies get chilly, dad. Particularly if they aren't…Is he breast fed?
DAD:	Uh, well… formula…most feedings.
SUIT LADY:	Ah. Well, bottle-babies are prone to cold. Say, well, Daddy, at least it's nice of you to take care of me for mommy today.
DAD:	I actually take him most days.
SUIT LADY:	Really.
DAD:	She works.
SUIT LADY:	How nice for you. (*to stroller*) Say, that's nice dad, but I need some socks.

SUIT LADY exits.

SPEAKER:	Hm. A pity.
DAD:	(*into stroller*) Say, we do just fine, Dad. Say, I don't want socks. Say, socks make me fart.
SPEAKER:	STOP IT. Hold it there. (*DAD freezes.*) So painful. Allow a vacuum of Command, and this is what happens. You must FILL your vacuum, gentlemen. Fill it! And of course, we all know the benefit Command brings. Why do women find it so compelling? Because they know it is the very essence of manhood. Science has

shown they can literally, physically smell Command. Roll it.

> *DAD is approached by a co-ed in jeans and a TANK-TOP.*

TANK-TOP: Oh, my god, he is so....

DAD: Yeah.

TANK-TOP: He is so...you must be so proud.

DAD: I am, actually.

TANK-TOP: Look at his hands.

DAD: Yeah...I'm pretty sure they're mine. I mean, he got my hands.

TANK-TOP: He does look like you.

DAD: You think? I wonder, sometimes. His eyes.

TANK-TOP: No, he definitely looks like you. And you take care of him?

DAD: Yeah, I mean, I'm doing a lot of freelance right now, so most days...

TANK-TOP: That is so great. I just think it's great that guys are doing this now.

DAD: Yeah, well, it's a challenge but...

TANK-TOP: Your wife must appreciate it a ton.

DAD: Uh...yeah...You know, my wife and I...it's fine. It's fine. Yeah.

TANK-TOP: (*indicating baby*) Can I?

DAD: Oh…yeah, sure…Let me…

> *DAD removes the baby from the stroller and hands it to TANK-TOP.*

TANK-TOP: Oh, my gosh, he's a load!

DAD: Yeah, he's a chunker. He's my little chunker.

> *TANK-TOP dandles the baby, jiggling him and cooing to him. Both ad lib, "Oh, boy, what a boy, bouncy, bouncy" etc. After a moment of enjoying the spectacle, DAD catches a whiff of something. He sniffs the air like a bloodhound. He tries to subtly sniff the baby's back. His suspicions are confirmed. He hangs his head.*

DAD: Uh…ma'am…I think I better…

TANK-TOP: Do you miss your daddy?

DAD: No, I just think he…

> *TANK-TOP smells it.*

TANK-TOP: Aw. Did you make a mess? Did you… (*TANK-TOP's smile dissolves as she inspects the baby. She's seen it. The Exxon Valdez of diapers. It's all over her.*) OH MY GOD! Oh my god! OH! God!

> *TANK-TOP holds the baby at arm's length. Dad quickly places the baby back in the stroller. TANK-TOP continues to ad lib disgust.*

DAD: Oh, god. God. I'm so sorry. I've got some wipes… (*DAD digs frantically in his bag. Finds the wipes. Pulls one out starts to clean her. She snatches them from him.*) It's the cloth diapers. My wife…

TANK-TOP: I have to go shower.

TANK-TOP exits in a huff. DAD pauses over the stroller. A beat. He smiles.

DAD: Your mother would be so proud.

DAD exits with stroller.

SPEAKER: As I said before, I believe that there are lessons to be learned from the ancients.

DAD enters pushing the stroller and carrying the baby's car seat. He arranges the chairs into a car, two up front and three in back. He steps back and then "opens" the door by sliding it back — obviously a minivan.

SPEAKER: Men, manhood is not new. Manhood is not a "nineties" phenomenon.

DAD crawls awkwardly into the back seat and attempts to install the car seat. The opponents are evenly matched, man and car seat. The battle rages throughout the backseat. DAD refers frequently to the directions.

SPEAKER: Millenniums have risen and set on manhood.

DAD: (*reading*) Thread vehicle belts through car seat belt slots.

SPEAKER: Manhood has evolved over millions of years.

The baby starts to wail.

DAD: Right there, buddy. Remove slack by pressing down firmly.

DAD climbs onto the car seat.

SPEAKER: Right here, right here in Austin manhood existed. And what form did manhood take for those eons and eons?

DAD: Buckle vehicle belt tightly.

SPEAKER: Freedom.

DAD: Check for secure installation.

SPEAKER: Freedom to move across the plains. Roaming, searching, hunting.

DAD: Check level indicator for proper installation.

DAD crawls out of the car to check level on the side of the seat. Baby continues wailing.

SPEAKER: This search, this quest, over the generations, sunk into the meat of maleness.

DAD: Right there, buddy. Red. (*reading the indicator*) If any part of the ball falls within red zones, injury, ejection or death may result. Jesus. So what…

SPEAKER: Manhood is movement.

DAD: If any part of the ball falls within red see your Playco dealer for base-leveling insert.

SPEAKER: Millions of years of conditioning tell us: You are a man. Move.

DAD: How are you supposed to get the fucking insert if you can't put the baby in the fucking seat to go to the fucking Playco?

The baby's wailing intensifies.

SPEAKER: Without the ability to move, to hunt…

DAD: Trapped.

SPEAKER: …you are no longer a man. (*a long silence*) Now I am not one to beat the Bible, but there is some scripture I'd like to share with you now…

DAD: JESUS! That's it!

DAD moves quickly to the tape recorder and turns it off. The SPEAKER freezes, Bible in hand. The crying stops.

DAD: God. What a penis.

DAD takes the Bible from SPEAKER's hands. Moves toward the car.

DAD: Why do I buy these tapes? (*to stroller*) Say, why do you buy those stupid tapes, Dad? (*DAD shoves the Bible under the car seat. Steps back to read the indicator.*) Green. And spiritually insured. (*DAD stands over the stroller.*) Come on, buddy, let's you and dad go for a ride.

He reaches for the baby. Blackout.

End of Play

OUT OF INK 2000: Speaking in Tongues

Ingredients:

1. The play must have a flash-forward in the plot.
2. The play must have a character who speaks a language other than English…which leads to complications.
3. The play must use one of the four elements in a really small or really big way. No in-between.

The ingredients were contributed by Michael Wright, author of <u>Playwriting in Process</u>, Michael Barnes, arts and society writer for the Austin-American Statesman, and playwright Naomi Iizuka.

The original production ran March 2-4 and 9-11, 2000 in the Gallery Theatre at Austin Community College, Rio Grande Campus with the following company:

Playwrights: Tim Bauer, Ron Berry, Monika Bustamante, Dan Dietz, Elizabeth D. Marquis, Clay Nichols, John Walch, Skipper Chong Warson, and Cyndi Williams

Directors: Meredith Baker, Christina J. Moore, Laura Somers, and David Yeakle

Performers: Chris Alonzo, Marita Delatorre, Sharon Elmore, Amie Elyn, Corey Gagne, Shannon Grounds, Christa Kimlicko Jones, Paula Knowles, Kathy Lagaza, Derek Mudd, Brian Stanton, Douglas Taylor, Lara Toner

Designers: Kenny Gall (set/props), James Timmins (lights), Skipper Chong Warson (sound)

Production Staff:
Stage Manager: Jennifer Rogers
Asst. Stage Manager: Tracey Herman

Light Board Operator: Toby Stoner
Sound Operator: Skipper Chong Warson

ScriptWorks Staff (then Austin Script Works):
Artistic Director: John Walch
Producing Director: Christina J. Moore
Member Representative: Cyndi Williams

SQUARE PEGS
John Walch
© 2000

CHARACTERS

PEGGY, *a lady of a certain age*
PEG, *another lady of a certain age*
BILL*, *a man who enjoys bumper-pool*
CALLER*, *off-stage voice*
**Played by the same actor*

SETTING

An empty room adjacent to the ballroom at Heritage Homes retirement village.

TIME

Valentine's Day.

In darkness, the sound of a swinging, foot-stomping, hand-clapping square dance with full musical accompaniment.

CALLER: Bow to your corner, bow to your own.
Three hands up and 'round you go,
Break it up with a do-si-do.
Pick it up and don't go slow.
Promenade once around the ring,
Everybody swing their pretty little thing.

Lights rise. A hand-crafted Valentine heart hangs from the ceiling. On it is scrawled the words: "Heritage Homes Valentines' Day Square Dance." Outlining the heart is a square box. PEGGY and PEG sit in chairs drinking punch. Two dress forms on casters stand silently beside them. The dress forms are got up in Western wear — flannel

> *shirts, kerchiefs, and cowboy hats. PEGGY rubs her feet.*

PEGGY: Bunions.

PEG: You shouldn't wear those shoes. Leather chafes.

PEGGY: Patent leather.

PEG: Huh?

PEGGY: My shoes. They're patent leather. You said just leather.

PEG: I said you shouldn't wear them.

PEGGY: Oh. *(Pause.)* The punch is splendid.

PEG: Last year you wore them and the same thing happened. Spent the rest of the month in your slippers. You should wear sensible shoes, Peggy.

PEGGY: I like the way they look. They match my handbag.

PEG: There's nobody here to look good for. And I'm not dancing with these dress forms again. It's impractical to square dance with these. Last year, when we had the ballroom theme, it wasn't so bad. You could just close your eyes, lean on them, and pretend. That was nice. To have something to lean against, to be able to pretend — but this, this is impossible. If we have a dance, we should have real partners.

PEGGY: Jack gave them to me. The shoes. Jack gave them to me.

PEG: Jack gave you shoes?

PEGGY: Jack gave me everything.

PEG: Henry gave me plenty, but he never would have done that. He was generous, but he never gave me shoes.

PEGGY: "Just for kicks," he said. It wasn't my birthday or anything.

PEG: I mean, how would he know if they fit? If they were comfortable?

PEGGY: "Just for kicks."

PEG: A man buying a woman shoes. That's not right. No wonder they pinch.

PEGGY: "Just for kicks."

PEG: You should get rid of those and get a new pair; a pair of shoes that fits who you are now.

PEGGY: (*a new thought*) Jack gave me these shoes.

PEG: I know…

PEGGY: Oh. (*Pause.*) The punch is splendid.

PEG: Yes, we have an excellent chef here.

> The CALLER's voice is heard off. Reality being different from the imagined, the CALLER's voice is much slower this time and the instructions are meted out with little rhythm and less enthusiasm.

CALLER: Honor to your partner …
Now swing that maid high … and … low
Allemande left … (no, no your other left, ladies)
leeeeeft with the corner, (There you go.)
Now you're on a do-si-do…

PEGGY: Time to get back out there. Don't want to get stuck with the forms for another dance.

PEG: I'm done with dancing. No more for me.

PEGGY: But the night's still young. And Bill Connerly's been fishing for a partner. Help me with my shoe, Peg?

PEG: I don't know what you see in him. He refuses to play bridge and just hangs out in the rec. room playing bumper-pool all day. Bumper-pool. Isn't that billiards for the insane?

PEGGY: I think he likes me.

PEG: Bill Connerly likes anything in a skirt, Peggy. He's a dog. Plus he has dirt under his fingernails. And if a man has dirt under his fingernails in a germ-free environment, then you know something's not right with him.

PEGGY: (*struggling with shoe*) Everyone says he and Frances Pennington are an item…But this afternoon…

PEG: Where do you think that dirt comes from? The outside courtyard is all Astroturf and we're not allowed any living plants on account of allergies. So where is that dirt coming from?

PEGGY: …this afternoon in the cafeteria…

PEG: Next time I see him in the rec. room playing pool, I'm just going to ask him point blank. I'm going to say. (*addressing one of the dress forms*) Hey, Bill.

BILL appears in a separate place with pool cue.

BILL: *Ita*, Peg?

PEG: What's the dirt on your dirt?

BILL: Memento mori.

PEG: What the hell does that mean, Bill? Talk straight.

BILL: Memento mori.

BILL disappears.

PEG: You never can get a straight answer out of that dirt rustler. Always talking Latin. Who's he think he's impressing? It's a dead language, for God's sake. It's depressing. Add that to the dirt, and he's just suspicious.

CALLER: Ladies make a left-hand star, (a star, good, good) now go full a — round the set...

PEGGY: He's still looking for a partner. Help me with my shoe, Peg.

PEG: I don't understand how you can see past the dirt?

PEGGY: Peg, please...

PEG: How you can see anything but the dirt, in fact.

Pause.

PEGGY: It's dirt from his wife's grave.

PEG: What?

PEGGY: The dirt is from his wife's grave. You're supposed to throw in a handful at the end.

PEG: Ashes to ashes. Dust to dust…

PEGGY: He couldn't do it. At the funeral. He kept the dirt in his hand. Put it in his coat pocket. When he came home, he put it in a jam jar. He sifts through it every day.

PEG: That's…morbid. Holding on like that. What must it do to a person to hold on for that long?

PEGGY: His wife was an original Rockette. Very beautiful. He showed me pictures.

PEG: Did he show you the dirt?

PEGGY: I told him we should put a seed in it and see what grows.

PEG: What did he say?

PEGGY: Dum spiro spero.

PEG: You can never get a straight answer out of him. *Dum spiro spero.*

PEGGY: "While there's life, there's hope." *(Pause.)* Then he cried. I think he likes me. Do you remember what it feels like to be liked? This afternoon in

	the cafeteria he gave me a Valentine that said: *Amo, Amas, Amat.*
PEG:	Peggy, he gave everyone a Valentine that said: *Amo, Amas, Amat*, even the staff.
PEGGY:	Did he give you one?
PEG:	Of course he gave me one.
PEGGY:	Oh.
CALLER:	Sashay to the music of the carousel, And promenade to the ting-a-ling of the ice-cream bell.
PEGGY:	He's still looking for me, Peg. Help me with my shoe.
PEG:	You shouldn't wear them; it's not practical. Your bunions.
PEGGY:	But how can I dance?
PEG:	Go back to your room and get your Hush Puppies.
PEGGY:	Please, Peg. There's no time. Do you remember what it feels like to be liked?
PEG:	Of course I do.
PEGGY:	I want to dance now.
PEG:	I'm just looking out for your best interest. I'm sorry.

CALLER: When you get back home, box-the-gnat. (No, no, not wheel-and-deal, box-the-gnat.)

PEGGY: Oh…look…

CALLER: (That's right, there you go, very good.) They call her Pussy Cat, oh Pussy Cat.

PEGGY: Look…now he's dancing the Pussy Cat with Frances Pennington.

Pause.

PEG: This punch is splendid.

PEGGY: I don't like it. No fizz.

PEG: No. I suppose not.

Pause.

PEGGY: I really thought he liked me.

PEG: He does like you.

PEGGY: No fizz.

PEG: Oh, come on, everybody likes you, Peggy. You're likable. Just like Henry. Everybody always liked Henry. I mean people liked me, but they really liked Henry. He was funny. Lots of fizz. He made jokes, made people smile. When they talked about us, they would say Henry *and Peg* this and Henry *and Peg* that. It was never Peg and Henry. Always Henry *and Peg*. Like I was a necessary fact — a given. A peg on which the coat of Henry hung. Not that I minded, I was comfortable there. But when he died, there was

	no more Henry *and Peg*. There was just Peg. Just Peg. And who likes just Peg?
PEGGY:	I like Peg.
PEG:	Then why do you go by Peggy?
PEGGY:	Peg is strong, solid, something to lean against. Always there for you.
PEG:	Please, Peg is not always there for you. If Peg were there for you she wouldn't have told you she got a Valentine from Bill Connerly. Peg didn't get a Valentine. Peg hasn't got a Valentine since the days of *Henry and*. So Peg is not there for you. Peg is alone. Peg is alone.
PEGGY:	Oh.

Pause.

CALLER:	All right ladies and gents, next one up is one of my favorites: *Pick a Doodle*. Everybody pick a partner for Pick a Doodle.
PEG:	I bet Bill Connerly is looking for a new dance partner.
PEGGY:	You think?
PEG:	Here, let me help you with your shoes.
PEGGY:	*(a new thought)* Jack gave them to me.
PEG:	They're very pretty.
PEGGY:	Thank you.

PEG takes PEGGY's other shoe off.

PEG:	But you shouldn't wear them.
PEGGY:	Peg, what are you doing?
PEG:	You don't need these old shoes to dance.
PEGGY:	But I can't dance in my stocking feet. What will Bill Connerly think?
PEG:	He'll think: *dum spiro spero*. And if he doesn't, then he's no better a partner than this dress form.
PEGGY:	But Jack gave them to me. The shoes. Jack gave them to me.
PEG:	Jack gave them to you just for kicks.
PEGGY:	That's right…he did. Jack gave them to me just for kicks.
PEG:	So what are you waiting for? Get out there and dance your bunions off.

They start laughing a little.

PEGGY:	Peg, you made a joke.
PEG:	I did. I did.
PEGGY:	That's not very practical.
PEG:	No, no it isn't.
CALLER:	Everybody got a sweetheart on their arm?
PEG:	You better go on and get out there.

PEGGY: But who will you dance with, Peg?

PEG: I'll be fine.

PEGGY: But the night's still young.

PEG: Yes, it is. The night is still young. Now go. (*PEGGY exits. PEG slips off her shoes and lines them next to PEGGY's.*) Dum spiro spero….

CALLER: Line 'em up, ladies and gents and get ready for Pick a Doodle.

PEG: *(to dress form)* Henry, may I request the honor of one last dance?

CALLER: All righty, then. Everybody on their toes and away we go. A one, two, a one-two-three!

The sound of a beautiful waltz fills the room. PEG leans against dress form and begins dancing. A slow waltz. As the lights begin to fade, she slowly opens the hand behind the dance form's back and lets sprinkle to the ground a handful of dirt.

PEG: Ashes to ashes. Dust to dust.

Lights fade to black. A pin spot remains on the two pairs of empty shoes for a beat of music and then fade all.

End of Play

OUT OF INK 2001: Boot Arias

Ingredients:

1. At some point in the play's action, one or more characters must suddenly and shockingly acknowledge the audience's presence.
2. Boots of some kind must figure prominently in the life of at least one of the characters.
3. The play must include a heart-wrenching aria that:
   a. speaks a great, deep truth.
   b. references any aspect of the ocean.
   c. stops, shatters or completely transforms the action/rhythm of the play.

(The aria can be sung, spoken, whispered, chanted, channeled, whatever.)

The ingredients were contributed by Mead Hunter, (then Director of Literary Programs at A.S.K. Theatre Projects), Scott Kanoff, (then Artistic Director of The State Theater Company), and playwright and ScriptWorks Core Alum, Lisa D'Amour.

The original production ran February 23-26, 2001 at the State Theater, 719 Congress Ave. in Austin with the following company:

Playwrights: Elena Carrillo, Vicki Caroline Cheatwood, Dan Dietz, Michael Kranes, Elizabeth D. Marquis, Marshall Ryan Maresca, Andrea Moon, and John Walch

Directors: Shoshana Gold, Cathy Hartenstein, Christina J. Moore, and Steve Shearer

Performers: Lowell Bartholomee, Mick D'Arcy, Melanie Dean, Travis Dean, Bethlyn Gerard, John Hoff, Amanda Poston, and Rebecca Robinson

Designers: Kenny Gall (sets), Phillip Ty Montoya (sound), William J. Stewart (lights)

Production Staff:
    Stage Manager: Ron Watson
    Technical Director: Kenny Gall
    Sound Operator: Phillip Ty Montoya
    Light Operator: William J. Stewart

ScriptWorks Staff (then Austin Script Works):
    Artistic Director: John Walch
    Producing Director: Christina J. Moore
    Member Representative: Cyndi Williams

HAZARD
John Walch
© 2001

CHARACTERS

GOVERNOR, *a governor of some large state, dressed for golf. He wears a pair of mismatched golf spikes, one white and one black.*

CADDIE, *a man with permanently sagging shoulders, older. He wears a pair of old tennis shoes.*

YOUNG MAN, *anonymous and faceless. He wears steel-toed work boots.*

SETTING

A golf tee — #18 — on a slight raised platform.

The GOVERNOR stands on the tee, behind him stands his CADDIE. The GOVERNOR is dressed in golf attire: tangerine orange shirt, kiwi green shorts, and a soiled visor. The outfit gives him the look of an escapee from a tropical fruit salad. He holds a putter in his hands. He tees up the ball, breathes, takes a practice swing, and lines up to the ball. As he prepares to swing, a YOUNG MAN enters and stands in the shadows directly in front of the tee. The YOUNG MAN wears a pair of heavy work boots. The GOVERNOR freezes.

GOVERNOR: Keep your eye on the ball... (*The GOVERNOR continues to stand frozen over the ball. He doesn't move and never looks out into the audience or at YOUNG MAN.*) Well...what is it?

CADDIE: Pardon, Governor?

GOVERNOR: I can hear you about to say something. It's very distracting and if you say it during my backswing it'll ruin everything. A man cannot be questioned during his backswing. Momentum is everything. So, what is it?

CADDIE: Just that…

GOVERNOR: What? Just that *what*?

CADDIE: Just that I thought you might want to reconsider.

GOVERNOR: Reconsider.

CADDIE: Yes, sir.

GOVERNOR: There's another one, isn't there?

CADDIE: Another, sir?

GOVERNOR: Another *one*!

CADDIE: Another club, sir? I thought you should reconsider your club selection, sir.

GOVERNOR: My club…

CADDIE: The putter. You don't drive with the putter. You drive with the driver —

GOVERNOR: And you putter around with the putter. Do you think that's where that word came from? To putter around? Or was the word there and the object followed?

CADDIE: I try not to dwell on things I can't resolve.

GOVERNOR: You're a caddie, this is the kind of information you should know: which came first, the verb putter or the noun putter?

CADDIE: God only knows, sir.

GOVERNOR: God. ... You believe there is one?

CADDIE: Oh yes, sir.

GOVERNOR: And this God of yours knows all. Knows which came first, action or object?

CADDIE: Yes, sir.

GOVERNOR: What else does this God of yours know?

CADDIE: That your chances of clearing the hazard are much better if you putt with the putter and drive with the driver.

GOVERNOR: What hazard?

CADDIE: The hazard right out there, sir.

GOVERNOR: Describe it to me.

CADDIE: You know it, sir. You play this course every Friday afternoon.

GOVERNOR: Describe it to me.

CADDIE: The 18th tee, the last hole, you know it well.

GOVERNOR: Describe it to me!

CADDIE: Look for yourself.

GOVERNOR: DESCRIBE IT TO ME!

> *Beat. CADDIE looks out into the audience. The GOVERNOR does not. Lights rise fully on YOUNG MAN as he addresses the audience.*

CADDIE: It's ... it's ...

YOUNG MAN: *(overlapping)* It's ... it's ... like this, okay? I got in this car with this guy I just met — Carl — and we were smoking some dirt weed and drinking and just driving out of the city till the car we stole ran out of gas. That's all I wanted to do, just get out of the city. Escape and run out of gas in the middle of nowhere and then I don't know, just figure it out. "Just figure it out as you go," that's what this guy Carl kept saying to me. And since I just met him and he had some weed, I thought: *why the hell not? (Beat.)* Now, I'm not saying I'm the best person — my judgment can be *questionable*. And I made some mistakes in my life, but I learned from them. I was cleaning up, looking for a job, but this one night, I felt like letting loose, getting out of the city, and this guy Carl stole this car, had a bag a weed and said: "hop in." So I did, but I'm no cop killer.

CADDIE: It's a water hazard, sir.

GOVERNOR: A water hazard?

CADDIE: A lake...

YOUNG MAN: So we run out of gas near this lake and we get out of the car, lay on the hood, and this guy Carl whips out a bag of PCP. We start getting rowdy, pounding on the car, turning up the radio, yelling, stupid shit like that. And I decide I wanna go for a swim, so I strip down and jump in the lake. My boots sitting there on the shore. My boots, they're steel-toed, okay, good for kicking in doors and you know, whatever. So, I'm swimming in the lake for I don't know how long, okay, I don't know how long I was swimming, but it was a long time.

GOVERNOR: What color is the water?

CADDIE: Black, sir. Ink black.

GOVERNOR: Ink black.

YOUNG MAN: Floating out there in that black water thinking I was some sort of swamp snake. There was no moon. No stars that night, just me — didn't know what Carl was doing — just me and that black water and for once, I felt free.

GOVERNOR: Never sign anything with a blue-ink pen.

CADDIE: Pardon, sir?

GOVERNOR: Always sign with black ink. It has authority, weight. That's a tip for you.

CADDIE: Thank you, sir ... Now, about the hazard.

GOVERNOR: Sign a document with a colored pen and it reeks of indecision. Like my golf shoes here.

CADDIE: Your shoes, sir?

GOVERNOR: In the locker room, I couldn't decide which pair I should wear, my black shoes or my white shoes, so I wore one of each.

CADDIE: Doesn't it affect your game?

GOVERNOR: On the contrary, I've never felt better. That moment of trying to decide between the black shoes and white shoes and then realizing: *I don't have to decide, I can wear both*. I've never felt so free.

YOUNG MAN: At some point, red lights start cutting through the darkness. And flashlight beams cutting 'cross the lake. The cops. Busted. Shit. A megaphone was calling me to come into shore.

CADDIE: We should continue sir, the hazard.

GOVERNOR: The hazard. The hazard. Can we just forget about the hazard for a minute!

CADDIE: But it's right there in front of you.

GOVERNOR: It's not!

CADDIE: It is and you have to cross it.... Sir...Governor...

YOUNG MAN: 'Fore I even got to shore, a bunch a cops fell on me in the shallows, started beating me, calling me all types of names, and yelling kill the cop killer. Cop killer? What? I didn't kill anyone. They pulled me into this brightly lit area that was all taped off and where this cop was laying in a pool of blood, his face all smashed in, and I was like: "what the fuck happened here?" And they said: "You know what happened you fuck and you're going to pay." Then they asked: "these your boots?"

CADDIE: ...Other players have started to back up behind us.

YOUNG MAN: And they were my boots — steel-toed — only the toes were covered with blood and I said: "yeah, but where's Carl."

GOVERNOR: Who?

YOUNG MAN: Carl, Carl. But they just kept beating me.

CADDIE: Other players. Other golfers are backing up behind us.

GOVERNOR: Expedite. We must expedite the process.

CADDIE: Yes, sir.

YOUNG MAN: The trial was a joke. Lasted a week.

GOVERNOR: It's not good for the course to be clogged with players. No one has fun then. To enjoy golf, play must proceed at an even, expeditious pace. At all costs.

CADDIE: (*holds driver out*) Exactly, sir. So, I suggest you take the driver.

YOUNG MAN: Lawyer they assigned me was in their pocket. First thing he said to me was: "if you confess, you might avoid the chair."

CADDIE: (*still holding driver*) Sir... your chances of clearing the hazard are much better with the driver.

YOUNG MAN: Confess what? I was a swamp creature. Carl did this.

GOVERNOR: I can clear it with the club I've selected. How far is it?

CADDIE: With all due respect, sir —

GOVERNOR: How far is it?

CADDIE: To the other side?

GOVERNOR: Of course to the other side!

CADDIE: 173 yards.

For the first time, the GOVERNOR looks out at the hazard.

GOVERNOR: 173 yards?…

YOUNG MAN: I never confessed. I couldn't confess to something I hadn't done. The plea for the appeal was denied.

GOVERNOR: Last week it was only a 170 yards.

CADDIE: It grew by three yards over the week.

YOUNG MAN: And they put me on death row.

GOVERNOR: The hazard grew?

YOUNG MAN: In one hour, I'm supposed to die by lethal injection.

CADDIE: Yes, it continues to grow, sir. When you first came here, Governor, it was a small little lake. Barely more than a puddle really: 15-20 yards across, but since you've been playing here it continues to grow.

YOUNG MAN: In one hour, a lethal dose of some poison that I don't know the name of will run through my veins. They say: *it's the most humane way to die.* They say: *you will feel no pain.* In one hour I will be dead unless…

GOVERNOR: Is there any stopping it?

CADDIE: I can't advise you on that, sir.

GOVERNOR: Is there any slowing it down?

CADDIE: I can't advise you on that either, sir.

GOVERNOR: What exactly can you advise me of!

CADDIE: I beg your pardon, sir?

YOUNG MAN: …A pardon has been sent to the Governor.

GOVERNOR: You're my caddie, you're supposed to be able to offer sound advice!

CADDIE: At this point sir, so late in the game, I would advise you only on your club selection. The driver.

YOUNG MAN: A stay of execution.

GOVERNOR: I'll use the club I selected. I won't change my mind, I won't go back, I won't.

CADDIE: Then maybe…

YOUNG MAN: If, after carefully reviewing the case, seeing the holes in the trial: the lack of hard evidence, if he sees the shadow of doubt, then he will decide to sign and maybe… maybe…

GOVERNOR: Maybe what!

YOUNG MAN: Maybe my life will be spared...

CADDIE: Maybe you should use a water ball.

GOVERNOR: A water ball?!

CADDIE: So, you don't lose your good ball in the hazard. Use an old cut ball. Minimize your loss.

GOVERNOR: You want me to use a water ball!

YOUNG MAN: (*pulling pen out of pocket*) Sign it please....

CADDIE: Governor, sir, you will lose something eventually. The hazard continues to grow and you cannot possibly clear it with the putter.

YOUNG MAN: Black ink...speaks of authority.

CADDIE: Sir, you have to make a decision, either take the driver or use a water ball.

YOUNG MAN: Sign it...please...

GOVERNOR: (*with even, but rising anger*) You insignificant, worthless little piece of human flotsam, how dare you suggest what or what I should not decide. I should take a pair of vise-grips and pull off one of your testicles, tee-it up, and see if I can clear the hazard with that! There's your water ball! How dare you force decisions on me, I play golf to escape, and here you are shoving water balls and drivers in my face! Always making me try to decide! Listen and listen carefully. The hazard is there. It's part of the game and I will face it using whatever club I pick, in whatever shoes I want, and using the best balls I got! And if a couple good balls are lost, then so be it. That is the price you pay for playing. That is the truth of the game. The way it is. Action before object. And if the hazard grows to 500 yards, a 1000 yards, 10,000 yards I will keep playing, because I know what is right. Because in my heart I know that to enjoy golf, play must proceed at an even, expeditious pace at all costs. At all costs!

CADDIE: At all costs.

YOUNG MAN: At all costs.

GOVERNOR: Now put that driver away and let's continue to play like civilized human beings. Do you understand?

CADDIE: Yes, sir...

GOVERNOR: And absolute silence during my back-swing, do you understand?

CADDIE: Momentum is everything.

GOVERNOR: Good.

> *CADDIE puts the driver back in bag. YOUNG MAN puts pen back in pocket. GOVERNOR lines up to the ball with the putter. Lights fade rapidly on the threesome.*

YOUNG MAN: It seems crazy to think that there's a final word in anything...especially my life...

GOVERNOR: Keep your eye on the ball....

YOUNG MAN: That one word could be my last. One word. What word will that be?... What word will that be?

In the middle of the GOVERNOR's backswing, the lights go completely black.

GOVERNOR: FORE!

End of Play

OUT OF INK 2002: Liquid Princesses

Ingredients:

1. The play should contain a monologue spoken by, or about, a princess.
2. A mysterious and unknown liquid substance leads to major complications in the plot.
3. The play must contain at least one element in the play's environment (setting, characters etc.) that completely contradicts the established order of things as presented by the playwright. i.e: Something that doesn't "fit" into the world of the play and would be completely foreign to it by all standards. In other words, it really has to stand out as not belonging in this play as such.

The ingredients were contributed by Rick DesRocher, (then Literary Manager at the Public Theatre/NYSF), Rick Roemer, (then Chair of Theatre Dept. at Southwestern University), and playwright Bridget Carpenter.

The original production ran June 7-10, 2002 at the Hideout Theater, 617 Congress Ave. in Austin with the following company:

Playwrights: Lowell Bartholomee, Ron Berry, Elena Carrillo, Vicki Caroline Cheatwood, Elizabeth D. Marquis, John Walch, Amanda Eyre Ward, and Cyndi Williams

Dramaturgs: Kimberly Burke, Greg Romero

Directors: Jennifer Haley, Ellie McBride, Christina J. Moore, Robi Polgar, and Steve Shearer

Performers: Marc Balester, Leigh Fisher, Bethlyn Gerard, Damien Gillen, Jennifer Hamilton, Flordelino

Langundino, Kathy Lagaza, Derek Mudd, Elia Nichols, and Douglas Taylor

Designers: Light Bastard Amber – Natalie George and Jennifer Rogers (lights), Star Costumes – Susan Kang (costumes), Nicole Smith (set), and Skipper Chong Warson (sound)

Production Staff:
Stage Manager: Patti Neff
Technical Director: Kenny Gall
Light Board Operator: Cleveland Dear
Sound Operator: Greg Janacek

ScriptWorks (then Austin Script Works) Staff:
Artistic Director: John Walch
Producing Director: Christina J. Moore
Member Representative: Cyndi Williams

THE LAST TIME COOPER TOOK MIDGE FISHING

Vicki Caroline Cheatwood
© 2002

CHARACTERS

COOPER
MIDGE, *his girlfriend*
THE FISH

SETTING

An old iron RR bridge, abandoned, over an isolated river. (Set should be suggested; perhaps an old ladder perched on two blocks.)

> *Lights up on MIDGE and COOPER sitting on the bridge. COOPER's fishing and drinking beer.*

MIDGE: There's more than one in the sea, you know.

COOPER: *(taking a drink)* Beer tastes funny.

MIDGE: You may think you got the market cornered, Cooper, but there's more than you. There is more than one fish in the sea. *(beat)* That's all I got to say.

COOPER: Beer tastes funny.

MIDGE: Johnny Kissee *(kuh-ZEE)*. Asked me ten times over before I run off with you. I could be living downtown Oklahoma City right now, in a skyscraper apartment, with a *terrace*. That's what it's called, you know. A *terrace*. *Terrace*. I could be having breakfast on a terrace every morning. Living the life of royalty. Driving a Cadillac Seville. Every year, a new Cadillac Seville. *White*.

	Red dirt or no red dirt, don't matter because Johnny'd have that car detailed for me once a week. Princess Grace'd never have it so good.
COOPER:	Why's the beer taste funny?
MIDGE:	I never had no business leaving Johnny and running off with a red-neck, red-dirt Okie. I was just scared, was all. Now, here I am, sitting out here on a rusted old bridge, freezing my hind-end off. For what? *(imitating COOPER)* "Come on, Midge, we'll have some'a that quality time you been yakking about." *(beat)* There's more than you in the sea, Cooper. Johnny's got four car lots now. The Ford, the Mercury, the Lincoln, *and Cadillac.* You'd hurl yourself off this bridge before you'd give me a new car. You'd rather see me dead behind the wheel of that Civic. *(imitating COOPER)* "Got nearly 200,000 miles on it, and still runs like a damn top." News to you, buster: it runs like a dad-blamed washing machine stuck in the spin cycle with the load all shifted. That's what it runs like. And don't tell me about those four new tires. I know they ain't new. Gayle Philpot told me you bought 'em off her car that she wrecked. *(imitating GAYLE)* "How you like riding on *my old tires*, Midge?" Go and tell *me* all new tires, and you know they're second-hand, and not even anonymous second-hand. You go and get 'em from the biggest mouth in Pottawatomie *(Pot-a-WHAT-toe-me)* county.
COOPER:	Beer tastes fun-ny. Like there's something been put in it. *(looks at her, suspicious)*
MIDGE:	There's nothing in that beer, 'cept your snoot. As usual. *(He drains the beer.)* Schlitz beer. Good

god. Who in the world except you drinks Schlitz beer anymore. Johnny Kissee never dranked nothing but Canadian Club and water. CC Waterback. *(sings, or repeats)* "CC Waterback…" Don't think I don't think of Johnny every time I hear that song. *(beat)* They hardly ever play it anymore.

COOPER: *(opens another beer, drinks deep)*…Sure tastes funny.

MIDGE: Please-to-GOD would you stop stop STOP saying that? You're like some old woman gone half-crazy, her mind playing the same things over and over and over. Why in this world I run off with you, I don't know. Stuck in the same old groove, going on and on and on and on and on. Saying the same old things again and again.

> *COOPER drinks deeply again, thinks it tastes funny, but doesn't say it. During the following, COOPER gets something on the line and whatever it is, it damn-near pulls him off the bridge before he can land it.*

MIDGE: Johnny Kissee wouldn't never have nothing to do with something as deadly dull as fishing. How can fishing be considered a sport, when all you do is sit on your can and freeze to death? I mean, if fishing was really a sport, wouldn't it be in the Olympics? Think about it, Cooper.
…Damn it. My brand-new jeans, and they're about ruined. Nothing like buying a new sweater and a new pair of jeans so we can celebrate our anniversary sitting on a railroad bridge in Nowhere, Oklahoma and freezing to death. I guess that's one thing. We'll *die* together. That's a stretch of quality time.

COOPER finally lands his catch: a large FEMALE FISH; MIDGE doesn't see it. She continues nagging on and on and on, underneath the dialogue.

FISH: Hello, Cooper!

COOPER: I knew it. There *was* something in that beer.

FISH: That's right, Cooper. There is. You're tripping on acid. Thanks to Mrs. Gerald Gerkin of Kenosha (KEN-o-shuh), Wisconsin. Mrs. Gerkin has been breaking into breweries all over the United States and injecting cans with a CIA-patented psycho-pharmaceutical recipe that she found on the Internet. This particular mixture is called "Dream Come True." It'll wear off in about six hours, and you'll be left with no major lasting side-effects - except that beer will now taste and behave like prune juice. Even if you develop a taste for it, every time you get drunk, you'll shit yourself, and sooner or later, you'll quit drinking.

COOPER: How come you don't show your bosoms?

FISH: I'm not a mermaid.

COOPER: A what?

FISH: I'm your dream-come-true, Cooper. A trophy bass big enough to get you your own fishing show.

COOPER: I'm gonna get my own fishing show?

FISH: Did I not say that this'll wear off in six hours?

COOPER: Well, then, to be fair, you should take off your top.

FISH: Cooper.

COOPER: If I don't get my own TV show, then at least I should see a little something.

FISH: I'm not a mammal, I'm a fish. *(He doesn't get it. FISH sighs.)* Fish don't have breasts.

COOPER: Well, damned if this don't suck.

FISH: You may not feel like thanking Mrs. Gerkin now, but your liver does. You were *this close* to wet-brain.

COOPER: *(beat, then)* Well. Gimme back my line, then.

FISH: You got a six-hour hallucination, and all you wanna do is fish?

COOPER: Might as well. *(at MIDGE)* What about…?

FISH: She'll leave you soon. On a Sunday evening. Sundays are extra-hard on Midge. The world's too quiet for her as it is.

COOPER: What if I was to give her some of this? *(holds up beer can. FISH shrugs, "try and see." COOPER offers MIDGE his beer.)*…Hey, taste this and tell me what you think might be wrong with it.

MIDGE: *(overlapping, in mid-sentence)* …and he sure wouldn't pulled that stunt you pulled at the Sirloin Stockade, pouring your ice tea in your salad — *(yanks the can out of his hand)* Oh, for God's sake, Cooper! Give me the damn …

MIDGE: *(takes a drink)* ...Why, it *don't* taste right. *(takes another drink)* Not bad, just a little...*(another drink)* a little fruity, kinda like Dr Pepper.

> *COOPER helps MIDGE take a BIG drink of the beer. She stops to stifle a belch. She giggles, tipsy. Immediately, COOPER falls to his death off the bridge. MIDGE looks up at the fish and sees Johnny Kissee —her old girlfriend.*

MIDGE: Johnny!

> *They embrace, look down off the bridge.*

FISH: He fell for it. *(chuckles at the pun)*

MIDGE: You always told me he was stupid, Johnny. *(strokes FISH'S hair)* My beautiful, beautiful girl....

FISH: Don't ever leave me again, Midge.

MIDGE: I won't. I'm not afraid anymore. People wanna talk, who gives a flip?

> *Big juicy kissy stuff from here on.*

FISH: Now, you know none of this is real. You know that...? *(MIDGE nods, sadly.)* ...So, how much was he worth?

MIDGE: Fifty grand in life insurance. Land and property won't bring more than $40K, all told. That's enough to get me the hell out of here.

FISH: Then what?

MIDGE: ...How long'll this last?

FISH: Six, seven hours.

                   MIDGE opens the cooler to reveal it's full of beer.

MIDGE: Is that…per can?

                   MIDGE and the FISH lie down on the bridge and make out.
                   Blackout.

End of Play

OUT OF INK 2003: Sitting Room Only

Ingredients:

1. The only furniture is one chair.
2. The notion of time running out, literally or figuratively.
3. The same question must be asked three times and answered three different ways.

The ingredients were contributed by Jason Neulander (then Artistic Director of Salvage Vanguard Theatre), Gary Garrison (then Executive Director of the Dramatists Guild), and playwright Karen Hartman.

The original production ran June 20-22 and 26-28 at Hyde Park Theatre, 511 W. 43rd St. in Austin with the following company:

Playwrights: Chris Alonzo, Tim Bauer, Monika Bustamante, Vicki Caroline Cheatwood, Jessica Hedrick, Marshall Ryan Maresca, Molly Rice, and Randy Wyatt

Dramaturgs: Elena Carrillo, David Gunderson

Directors: Ellie McBride, Christina J. Moore, Kevin Remington, and Deanna Shoemaker

Performers: Ken Bradley, Sondra Crawford, Michael D'Alonzo, Bethlyn Gerard, Heather Hanna, Yasmin Kittles, Derek Mudd, Rebecca Robinson, and Jose Marenco Villarreal

Designers: Theada Bellenger (sets/props), Light Bastard Amber – Natalie George and Jennifer Rogers (lighting), Marisa Pisano (costumes), and Bryan Schneider (sound)

Production Staff:
- Stage Manager: Patti Neff
- Asst. Stage Manager: Casey Kleam
- Light Board Operator: Lindsay Bright
- Sound Operator: Cris Edwards
- Deck Crew: Theada Bellenger

ScriptWorks staff (then Austin Script Works):
- Artistic Director: Dan Dietz
- Producing Director: Christina J. Moore
- Member Representative: Cyndi Williams

THE CHAIR
Molly Beth Brenner
©2003

CHARACTERS

SYLVIA, *14*
JENNY, *12*

Two young girls are lying on the floor with blankets and pillows. SYLVIA is fourteen. JENNY is twelve. There is a chair sitting against the wall. There is no other furniture.

Long pause. They lay motionless in the dark.

JENNY: *(whispering)* Are you awake?

SYLVIA: No.

Pause.

JENNY: Sylvia?

SYLVIA snores.

JENNY: Shut up. You are too awake.

SYLVIA: What do you *want*?

JENNY: I was just thinking.

SYLVIA: Oh Jesus. Here we go.

JENNY: No, really. Do you ever think about the fact that we don't go to church?

SYLVIA: No.

JENNY: You don't?

SYLVIA: No.

JENNY: Don't you ever wish we went?

SYLVIA: Why would I wish that?

JENNY: I dunno. There's music.

SYLVIA: Music?

JENNY: Yeah, you know. Singing and all that.

SYLVIA: So what? You can just turn on the damn radio and get singing.

JENNY: Yeah, but church has singing and Jesus. And God.

SYLVIA: So what?

JENNY: Don't you like God? Or Jesus, even? You have to like Jesus.

SYLVIA: Who says?

JENNY: You go to hell if you don't like Jesus.

SYLVIA: That's just a bunch of crap.

JENNY: How do you know?

Pause.

I like Jesus.

Pause.

I don't want to go to hell.

SYLVIA: You're not going to hell, dumbass.

JENNY: How do you know?

SYLVIA: You're just not. I think you have to be at least 20 to go to hell, anyway.

JENNY: Really?

SYLVIA: Yes. Now go to sleep.

JENNY: So, you're saying I only have eight years to figure out how not to go to hell, all by myself, without going to church? How am I going to do that?

Long pause.

Sylvia?

Pause.

Are you awake?

SYLVIA: What the hell is it?

JENNY: Why do you think God gave girls what they have, and boys what they have?

SYLVIA: What do you mean?

JENNY: You know. Like, our bodies. How come boys get to have something that sticks out, and girls have to have something that gets — stuck into?

SYLVIA: Don't be a weirdo.

JENNY: I wish I was a boy.

SYLVIA: Yeah, don't we all.

JENNY: If I was a boy, I'd go around sticking my thing into everything, just to see what it felt like. *(giggles)* Not people, though. Just things. Melons. Feather pillows. Tapioca! *(laughs)*

SYLVIA: *(laughing)* God, what's wrong with you?

JENNY: I wonder if it's like having another finger.

SYLVIA: I don't know. Another finger'd probly be more useful.

JENNY: Sylvia?

SYLVIA: Yeah.

JENNY: I hate boys.

SYLVIA: I know.

Pause.

JENNY: You know what I really wish I had, though? A tail. Like, one that could hold onto things. It'd be like having another arm. You could do your homework faster than everyone else. You'd get straight A's. And then, if someone was trying to get you, you could fight with your hands and your tail could grab a rock and smash them on the head from behind. You'd have to get special pants made, though.

SYLVIA: Oh, didn't Ma tell you?

JENNY: What?

SYLVIA: I thought for sure she woulda told you by now.

JENNY: *What?*

SYLVIA: You did have a tail. When you were born.

Pause.

JENNY: Ha, ha.

SYLVIA: Yeah. A nice, long, smooth one. Like a rat's tail, kind of. But cute.

JENNY: Shut up.

SYLVIA: I could hold out my little finger and your little tail would just curl around it, sweet as you please.

JENNY: Nuh-uh.

SYLVIA: Ma was freaked out at first, but the doctor said it happens like that sometimes. Every now and then.

JENNY: Are you for real?

SYLVIA: I'm serious. Like, one out of ten thousand babies are born with one.

JENNY: For real?

SYLVIA: Yeah.

JENNY: Well, how come I don't still have one?

SYLVIA: They cut it off, stupid. Ma didn't want to make *(starts cracking up)* all those special pants for you.

JENNY: You are so mean.

SYLVIA: *(laughing)* A tail! For Chrissakes!

> *There is a noise outside. SYLVIA raises her head. They both freeze.*

JENNY: What was that?

SYLVIA: Just the cat, I think. Go back to sleep.

JENNY: Maybe he won't come home tonight.

SYLVIA: Maybe.

> *Long pause.*

JENNY: Sylvia?

SYLVIA: What?

JENNY: Do you think God likes me?

SYLVIA: What the hell kind of question is that?

JENNY: I dunno.

SYLVIA: How would I know?

> *Pause.*

Yes. I think God likes you.

JENNY: What about Jesus?

SYLVIA: If God likes you, what the hell does Jesus have to say about it?

JENNY: I dunno. They're two different people, right?

SYLVIA: Yeah, but Jesus is the son. If God likes you, Jesus has to too.

JENNY: Oh yeah. "He's seated at the right hand of the father," like from church at Gramma's. I wonder what he's sitting on. A big throne, probably. A huge, beautiful throne with all kinds of intricate carving, all polished shiny by the saints, and with a big soft red pillow so he can stay comfortable. He probly has one of those big sticks too, like kings hold.

SYLVIA: A scepter.

JENNY: Yeah.

I wonder if he gets to walk around from time to time. Or if he just sits there, day after day. I wonder if he gets bored.

I hope you're right. I hope Jesus likes me.

I wish Jesus was my dad.

SYLVIA: Jesus is nobody's dad.

JENNY: I wish he was mine. And just mine. I wouldn't share him with anybody else.

Pause.

Except maybe you.

SYLVIA: Thanks.

JENNY: If you're nice to me.

> *Front door opens in another room. Both the girls inhale and fall silent quickly. We can hear heavy footsteps in the other room, thumps, mumbling.*
>
> *Long, long pause.*

JENNY: Sylvia?

SYLVIA: *(desperate)* Jenny, you *have* to be quiet now.

JENNY: *(looking at the chair)* Do you really think it'll keep him out?

> *Pause.*

Are you awake?

> *Pause.*

Sylvia?

End of Play

OUT OF INK 2004:
Of Superheroes and Seductions

Ingredients:

1. A seduction (large or small).
2. An ordinary object which a character owns, steals or inherits that they believe possesses profound religious, magical or spiritual significance.
3. A superhero that figures prominently in the lives of one of the characters.

The ingredients were contributed by playwright Carlos Murillo, Michelle Polgar (then Associate Artistic Director of the State Theater), and Amy Wegener (then Literary Manager of the Guthrie Theatre).

The original production ran April 14-18, 2004 at the State Theater, 719 Congress Ave. in Austin with the following company:

Playwrights: Rebecca Beegle, Dan Dietz, Amparo Garcia-Crow, Kendall Lynch, Kirk Lynn, Marshall Maresca, Bruce Rousseau, and Skipper Chong Warson

Directors: Sonnet Blanton, Emily Fordyce, Ellie McBride, and Christina J. Moore

Dramaturgs: Abi Basch, Monika Bustamante

Designers: Pam Fletcher-Friday (costumes), Light Bastard Amber – Natalie George and Jennifer Rogers (lighting), Ben Mettin (sound), Chase Staggs (set)

Performers: David DuBose, Jude Hickey, Yasmin Kittles, Casey Kleam, Laetitia Leon, Carra Martinez, Derek Mudd, Peck Phillips, Amanda Poston, Rupert Reyes, and Jose Villarreal

Production Staff:
        Stage Manager: Rebecca Gutierrez
        Asst. Stage Manager: Casey Kleam
        Prop Master/Deck Crew: Randy Wyatt
        Deck Crew: Cleveland Dear

ScriptWorks Staff (then Austin Script Works):
        Artistic Director: Dan Dietz
        Producing Director: Christina J. Moore
        Member Representative: Cyndi Williams

KRYPTONITE
Dan Dietz
© 2004

CHARACTERS

HARRIS, *about 30*
TODD, *mid-30s*
DAD, about 60

SETTING

A cemetery. Night.

Grunts in the dark, like someone straining against a huge weight. Then a loud yell of effort, followed by heavy breathing. Moonlight slowly rises on a cemetery. There is a large, awkwardly-dug hole in front of one of the headstones with a huge mound of dirt beside it. Out of the hole juts the end of a funeral casket. And on top of the casket, silhouetted in the moonlight, stands HARRIS. He's about 30, with scraggly hair, a leather jacket, biker boots, and eyes that sparkle like a child's. He breathes for a moment in silence. Then, in a rush, he speaks.

HARRIS: When I was six years old I fell off the top of a building, I fell, fell far, falling, and fast, when I was six years old I fell off the top of a residential building, off the roof garden at the top of a very tall building downtown, fell far falling, when I was six I fell and fell far and when I got to the bottom, almost to the very bottom of the far I had to fall, with the concrete zooming zooming toward me like a wall the size of the whole planet, the lines and crosswalks spinning and winking at me in this horrible semaphore, when I was almost there at the end of that far I had to fall, the sidewalk rushing up fast far fall, FATHER! Caught me. By the back of my green wool sweater. Held me in one hand as easy as a cat carries its young. And flew me back up to the top.

No one saw it. It happened in a blink. Speed of light.

We never spoke of it.

> *HARRIS leaps into the hole and disappears. A flashlight beam bobs and dances over the space, and TODD — clean-cut, mid-30s — runs in.*

TODD: I don't believe it! I do not believe this. You did it. You're doing it.

HARRIS: (*calling up from the hole*) It's done!

> *A shovel flies up out of the hole, past TODD.*

TODD: Harris. Come out of the hole and put it back.

HARRIS: Put what back?

TODD: Everything. The casket, the dirt, the whole…hole! Put the hole back!

HARRIS: Put the hole back?

TODD: Yes!

> *HARRIS climbs up the casket and perches on top.*

HARRIS: (*gleeful*) You can't put a hole back, Todd. You're asking the impossible. I'm just an ordinary man.

TODD: (*kicking the pile of dirt*) You know what I mean!

HARRIS: Hey! Don't mess with that. I made it, it's mine.

TODD: It's not yours. It's his. Now put it back.

HARRIS: Why?

TODD: Because it's a crime.

HARRIS: What are you gonna do, Mr. Big City Law Firm, prosecute me? Prosecute your own flesh and blood?

TODD: Then because it's sick.

HARRIS: Anything you don't understand, you call sick. Punk rock, sick. Leather bars, sick. Green Party —

TODD: Fine! Then because it's our father.

HARRIS: I know it's our father. Do you think I'd dig up the body of a total stranger?

TODD: You shouldn't be digging up bodies at all! Bodies die. Bodies get buried. And bodies stay there. It's a one-way transaction. You go down, you don't go up again.

HARRIS: When I was six years old I fell off the top of a building —

TODD: Not that again.

HARRIS: I fell, fell far, falling, and fast —

TODD: Is that what this is about?

HARRIS: When I was six years old —

TODD: You imagined that.

HARRIS: Impossible.

TODD: You imagined impossible things all the time. Which made it very difficult for me, your older brother, to impress you. I hated you for that.

HARRIS: Do you hate me now?

TODD: If you put the hole back, I will try not to hate you.

HARRIS: Impossible.

TODD: Stop saying that.

HARRIS: I'm on a mission.

TODD: You're on something.

HARRIS: Positive identification. Mysteries resolved. Doors unlocked. The keys of the universe —

TODD: HARRIS! OUR FATHER WAS NOT SUPERMAN!

Pause.

HARRIS: You can't prove that.

TODD: The burden of proof is not on ME! I'm not making a case for the impossible! Shit. Now you've got me saying it.

HARRIS: Fact: Dad was a newspaper reporter. Some might even have described him as…mild-mannered.

TODD: Not me.

HARRIS: Fact: He was adopted by a family in the Midwest who found him in a field as a meteor shower streaked above their heads. Fact: he was a high school football star with a throwing arm that the papers called nothing short of imp —

TODD: Don't say it!

HARRIS: Fact: he married a hard-nosed, fast-talking female reporter.

TODD: Who left him — left us — about which time, I recall, your imagination shifted into overdrive.

HARRIS: Fact: he disappeared for stretches of time and refused to ever tell us where he went or why.

TODD: He was covering wars in crappy little countries with no names. He was a foreign correspondent who saw too much and therefore drank too much.

HARRIS: Was he, though, Todd? Was he really?

TODD: I thought you were over this. I thought you got past this fantasy when you were like nine. Because that's what this is, Harris: fantasy, not —

HARRIS: Fact.

> *HARRIS reaches in his pocket and pulls out a balled-up handkerchief. He unwraps it and reveals a luminous green rock. TODD's eyes go wide.*

TODD: Where did you get that?

HARRIS: From his bedside table. Tucked away in a drawer. Where I'm sure it's been for years.

TODD: And you're telling me you think it's…

HARRIS: I was picking up his stuff this morning. Trying to do the whole "Keep Pile/Throwaway Pile" thing like you told me. And I yanked open the drawer…and this soft green glow rose up into my face. I reached into the glow and pulled out…this. And suddenly, I felt the strength begin to ooze from my muscles. Like when you prick the skin of a turkey to see if it's done. Just coming out and out, my energy draining out through my skin, through my hands, into the rock. *Faster than a*, I thought. *More powerful than a. Able to*, I thought. *Single bound.*

TODD: Harris. Listen to me. That's nothing but a stupid St. Patrick's Day souvenir he got from Uncle Phil. See those glue spots? That's where the little sign used to be that said "Blarney Stone." It's a joke. It's a gag.

HARRIS: It's proof. And it means there's hope. He could have been so drained of his solar energy by this little rock that he appeared, to the best efforts of Earth science, to be dead. But in reality, he

	was just waiting for the sun's yellow radiation to shine on his body so he could replenish himself.
TODD:	It's not fucking Kryptonite. Here. I bet the paint scratches off.
HARRIS:	Don't touch it! Are you crazy?!
TODD:	Why not? If it's really Kryptonite, it'll only affect him, right? He's "Superman," not me.
HARRIS:	We're his sons. His weaknesses are ours.
TODD:	Then what about his strengths? Catch any bullets between your teeth lately?
	HARRIS wraps the rock up and puts it back in his pocket.
HARRIS:	There was no sun in that hospital room. You wouldn't know that. You never came to see him. I was there for days, weeks at a time. I was in that room with him right to the end.
TODD:	And who was paying for that room, huh? For the drugs, the chemo? And then for the life support? You, who's been fired from every bar in New York? I carried my share, so don't get all high and mighty with me.
HARRIS:	No sun. Just the shadow of the building next door leaking through the window. Cancer? Don't make me laugh. Never sick a day in his life and then "cancer?" Someone planted this. Someone like —
TODD:	Please don't say Lex Luthor, please don't say Lex Luthor…

HARRIS: You can't prove I'm wrong!

TODD: How much?

HARRIS: What are you talking about?

TODD: How much did you do before you came out here?

HARRIS: That is so typical of you. Every time I feel passionate about something, you accuse me of —

TODD: HOW MUCH?

Beat.

HARRIS: A couple lines. Little ones. Jesus, my dad just died, cut me some fucking…No. You know what? Fuck you. Because you never, I mean —

TODD: I'm sorry, I thought I made it clear to you I don't listen to babbling cokeheads.

HARRIS: FUCK YOU!

TODD: Explains how you managed to dig a hole like this all by yourself.

HARRIS: Exactly! I needed it to combat the effects of the Kryptonite! And now, I'm gonna get what I came for.

HARRIS grabs a crowbar and starts trying to pry open the casket.

TODD: Harris, stop it! Stop it!

TODD grabs him, the two wrestle with each other.

HARRIS: Let me go! Get offa me! (*TODD wrenches the crowbar from HARRIS' hands.*) Give that back!

TODD: Forget it!

HARRIS: Come on, Todd! He just needs some light! We'll open him up and wait for morning. That's all he needs and then he'll come back!

TODD: It's over.

HARRIS: Why? What do you care?

TODD: It's wrong.

HARRIS: No.

TODD: It's sick!

HARRIS: No!

TODD: I'M NOT LOOKING AT THAT MOTHERFUCKER'S FACE EVER AGAIN!

Pause. The two men stare at each other, breathing heavily.

TODD: You just took it, you know? Year after year. From the day Mom left to the day he died. Every insult, every hand across the face, the bruises and welts, you took it. At least I fought him. At least I tried.

HARRIS: And you lost every time. Fighting him was —

TODD: Impossible, right? Yeah. So you took it. And smiled. And an hour later, you'd be cuddling up in his lap.

HARRIS: Because I knew. I knew it would all make sense someday. He could be so kind. Gentle. Animals. The way he was around animals. Cupping a hurt bird in the tail of his shirt, carrying its broken body into the house, all the while never laying a finger on it. Can you imagine what it must be like? Having that power humming under your skin? And then having to go through life touching people? Of course, you'd yell at them. You'd do whatever it took to keep them away.

TODD: Harris.

HARRIS: Think about it! How many houses torn off their foundations before you learn how to open a door? How many fingers crushed before you can hold a hand? The wounded you must leave in your wake. Like a trail of refugees. Seeking asylum. From you. You tell them, "Don't run. Please. This isn't a war. I'm not a war. I'm just living. That's all I'm trying to do. I'm here to save you."

TODD: *(genuine, concerned)* Harris. You have got to get some help.

HARRIS: Shut up.

TODD: I mean it. You need to get off the drugs, maybe get yourself some therapy.

HARRIS: You always treat me this way.

TODD: Please. I can give you the number of a —

HARRIS: NO!

HARRIS lunges for the crowbar. TODD swings it defensively, and it hits HARRIS in the head. He stumbles back and stares at TODD. A faint smile comes over HARRIS' face. Then he collapses.

TODD: Oh my god. Harris? Harris, I'm sorry. Please. (*TODD shakes him. HARRIS remains limp.*) Come on. Wake up! I didn't mean to. Okay. Okay. I'm getting help. Just stay here. Hold on.

TODD runs offstage. Quiet for a moment. Then with a POP-POP-CRRRACK! the lid of the casket flies open. Slowly, DAD climbs out. He is tall, rail-thin, and definitely dead. But something about his looks and bearing makes you see how maybe once, long ago, you might have thought he looked like Superman. He walks over to HARRIS and looks down at him. Then, like it's nothing at all, DAD picks HARRIS up by the collar of his jacket and holds him aloft.

DAD: It's time, Harris. Come with me. When you awake, you'll be in midair. Whooshing through cumuli. You'll be inside the weather. You'll see the planet revolve beneath you. Watch the sun tease itself over the edge and into your eyes. I always wanted to give that to you. Crack the Earth open like an egg. Pour its riches at your feet. But things get in the way. How can I tell you? You fly around the world often enough and the entire planet begins to shrink. The people swarming over its surface, over each other. You wonder what the point is, bearing witness to it all. The sun rises over the Earth's curve. And it's nothing but a golden hole you want so badly to fall into I'm gonna have to bring you back. But for a second, I can show you this. It's not an answer, really. More like a direction.

HARRIS: (*mumbling, unconscious*) Up…up…

DAD: Exactly. And away.

> *DAD braces his legs, as if about to leap straight into the sky. Blackout.*

End of Play

OUT OF INK 2005: Talk Doesn't Cook Rice

Ingredients:

1. Chalk.
2. A broken expectation.
3. The Chinese proverb, "Talk doesn't cook rice."

These elements were contributed by playwright Alice Tuan, SITI Company member, J. Ed Araiza, and Zach Scott Artistic Director, Dave Steakley.

The original production ran May 12-16 at the Blue Theater, 916 Springdale Rd. with the following company:

Playwrights: Lowell Bartholomee, Abi Basch, Vicki Caroline Cheatwood, Deni Krueger, Isabella Russell-Ides, Steven Salzman, Hank Schwemmer, and C. Denby Swanson

Dramaturgs: Amparo Garcia-Crow, Kirk Lynn

Directors: Emily Fordyce, Ellie McBride, and Sharon Sparlin

Performers: Tamara Beland, Elizabeth Doss, David DuBose, Sharon Elmore, Adriene Mishler, Todd Porter, Chris Sykes, and Jose Villarreal

Designers: Lowell Bartholomee, Emily Fordyce, Phillip Owen (sound), Light Bastard Amber – Natalie George and Jennifer Rogers (lighting), Adam Sekular (projections), Sarah Smiley (sets/props)

Production Staff:
Stage Manager: Jennifer Hamilton
Asst. Stage Manager: Sarah Smiley
Light Board Operator: Jess Aiken

ScriptWorks staff (Austin Script Works then):
    Artistic Director: C. Denby Swanson
    Producing Director: Christina J. Moore
    Member Representative: Rebecca Beegle

FAMILY PLANNING
Steven Salzman
© 2005

CHARACTERS

IRENE NESBITT, *(mid-sixties) Sensible, practical, always knows best. Experience has left her disillusioned. Finds strength in her faith.*

MARLEY, *(late twenties) Innocent. New age-y and noble, clings to youthful idealism, enjoys being the mediator, the diplomat, too eager to please.*

TERESA NESBITT, *(late thirties/early forties) Hard-headed, impulsive, rebellious. Loves the attention that comes with ruffling feathers.*

DR. GOLDBERG, *(mid-forties) Established, clinical. Willing to rise above others shortcomings. Her bedside manner is warm, but guarded. Not overly sentimental.*

SCENE ONE

Yesterday.
The Garden.

> *IRENE kneels by a small olive tree. She works white powder into the soil around it. She stops and stares away.*
>
> *Throughout the following scene, IRENE never looks directly at MARLEY:*
>
> *MARLEY enters.*

IRENE: Are you angry with me?

> *MARLEY shrugs.*

IRENE: I should call first. Someday I'll learn

> *IRENE continues gardening.*

IRENE: When I was a missionary. There was a couple. In a hut. She was in labor. A filthy hut. It was horrible, to bring an infant into such squalor. The woman was young, so small. Big lungs though. How she screamed. I tried to talk some sense into her, but the translator wasn't with me. Well, the baby came. A girl. So white, she was blue. Like a ghost. Like a holy ghost.

The man barked at me. The woman closed her eyes. He swept up the child. I followed him out of the hut and toward the river. I was so naive. I thought, "Hallelujah - he's going to baptize her."

When I had Teresa. It was so, sterile. I never felt a thing.

MARLEY: What are you doing?

IRENE motions with her trowel.

IRENE: The soil's bad. I had it tested.

MARLEY: I didn't ask for your help.

IRENE: Nothing will grow in this.

MARLEY: We're organic.

IRENE: It's limestone, not anthrax. Just chalk, Jesus Christ, what could be more natural.

MARLEY: We don't believe in …

IRENE: Can you never let me win? Sometimes I know what I'm talking about.

MARLEY:	Care for some tea. Oolong, or Jasmine?
IRENE:	Marley, do you hate me? For interfering.
MARLEY:	You're not responsible. Her body, her choice.
IRENE:	Now you sound like Teresa. She might be here if I hadn't talked her out of it. The procedure.
MARLEY:	You didn't. When did you ever talk her out of anything? Talk is cheap. Talk doesn't cook rice.
IRENE:	Where'd you get that?
MARLEY:	Read it off a tea box. Come inside?
IRENE:	I'm fertilizing. Maybe next season, something nice will grow. Mark my word.

SCENE TWO

Three months ago.
Medical Office. An exam table, a chair or two. A small supply table.

TERESA reclines on exam table.

IRENE enters. She carries a large handbag.

IRENE:	Teresa, there you are. They told me room three, but it's a black couple in there.
TERESA:	Mother. What are you…why are you here?
IRENE:	You're welcome. I couldn't let you do this alone.
TERESA:	I'm not alone.

IRENE: I don't see your…friend.

> *MARLEY enters carrying two juice boxes.*

MARLEY: All I found was apple juice. Miz. Nesbitt. What a pleasure.

IRENE: Misses.

TERESA: Mother's just leaving.

IRENE: What? I'm supposed to miss everything. What if they need to contact a family member?

MARLEY: Got that covered. Thanks.

TERESA: Please get her out.

IRENE: God forbid I should get a peek at my own grandchild.

MARLEY: They'll print the sonogram. We can show it to you.

> *IRENE fishes in her hand bag, takes out a photo and hands it to TERESA.*

TERESA: What?

IRENE: If I die before he's born you can show him my picture. See, I'm on the Great Wall.

TERESA: We should be so lucky.

IRENE: Come again?

MARLEY: Hon'. Remember? Inclusion?

TERESA: *(to IRENE)* If you promise to keep quiet.

IRENE: Not a word. It's like I'm in church.

> *IRENE takes a seat in the corner.*
>
> *MARLEY tends to TERESA's comfort.*
>
> *A beat.*
>
> *IRENE looks around the room.*

IRENE: So. This is a Jewish Hospital. You know when I married your father, he had to take a pledge that our off-spring would be raised in the faith.

TERESA: Well, since we can't get married, I guess that nonsense doesn't apply now does it.

IRENE: That's nice. I'm nervous as heck. Go ahead. Antagonize me.

TERESA: It's a routine sonogram.

IRENE: There's nothing routine about it. In my day we didn't have sonograms. We just had to go on faith.

TERESA: Well here we are. In the twenty-first century and they're fairly routine.

IRENE: It's not natural. Not God's plan.

TERESA: We've been through this. Plans change. Look, there's really no reason for you to be here.

MARLEY: She's excited for us. Let her stay.

IRENE: Thank you, Marley.

>   *IRENE reaches in her bag. She extracts three or four boxes of tea and sets them on the table.*

IRENE: I brought some tea. It's Oriental. Mandarin, Oolong, Darjeeling.

MARLEY: Very thoughtful.

IRENE: It's soothing.

TERESA: I'm here to look at the inside of my uterus. Not for a tea party.

IRENE: It's not for you. And the polite word is womb. Marley, find me some boiling water.

TERESA: She's not the waitress.

IRENE Of course not dear. I forget where we are. The Sisters of Mercy have carafes of hot water in all the exam rooms.

TERESA: The Sisters of Mercy don't list two women on the birth certificate.

MARLEY: Hon', please. Your blood pressure.

>   *DOCTOR GOLDBERG enters, carries a medical chart.*

GOLDBERG: Sorry for the delay

IRENE: Hot water, please. And tell the doctor we'll see him now.

TERESA: Doctor Goldberg, Irene Nesbitt.

IRENE stands, extends her hand.

IRENE: Hello. I'm not a lesbian. I'm widowed. By her Father.

GOLDBERG. Congratulations, Mrs. Nesbitt.

IRENE: Irene. And to you. Your people have come so far.

GOLDBERG. Yes. Now if you'll excuse us, we'll be a few minutes.

IRENE: Mercy. I'm not welcomed?

GOLDBERG looks to TERESA and MARLEY.

TERESA: Only if you're quiet. That means no talking.

IRENE collects her tea boxes and sits in a corner.

GOLDBERG listens to TERESA's belly with a stethoscope.

IRENE opens and closes the flaps on the tea boxes, dropping them, picking them up - creating her own disturbance.

GOLDBERG, TERESA and MARLEY stare at her.

IRENE: *(explaining)* They're very inspirational. *(She reads a quote.)* "The true mystery of the world is the visible, not the invisible." Oscar Wilde.

TERESA: I said no talking.

IRENE: *(confidentially to GOLDBERG)* Always has to have the last word.

TERESA: Mother, out.

> *IRENE "locks" her lips and throws away the key.*

GOLDBERG: So, the good news is that many of the results are normal.

IRENE: *(reading the box)* Oh. Look, it's Kosher.

GOLDBERG: But there are some minor irregularities. As a precaution, I'm going to order some further tests.

MARLEY: What irregularities?

GOLDBERG: The tests show slight abnormalities.

TERESA: How slight?

MARLEY: With Teresa or the baby?

GOLDBERG: Sometimes these things are just false positives. Blips. I don't want to alarm anyone. The sooner we verify things the more…options we'll have.

TERESA: Can we still do the sonogram?

GOLDBERG: It's best to wait.

IRENE: *(reads a quote)* "What doesn't kill me makes me stronger." Albert Camus.

TERESA: Mother, zip it.

IRENE: It soothes me.

MARLEY: Maybe this isn't the right time.

IRENE: *(reads)* "Take your life in your hands and what happens? A terrible thing: no one to blame." Mark my word, you sometimes find wisdom in surprising places. Excuse me, doctor.

IRENE exits.

SCENE THREE

Three months earlier.
The Garden.

TERESA sits. IRENE stands next to her holding the olive tree. Its roots are wrapped in burlap.

IRENE: What does that mean? "We're trying"?

MARLEY enters with a tea tray, sets it down. Sits next to TERESA.

TERESA: Marley and I are trying to get pregnant.

IRENE drops the plant.

IRENE: I'm going to lose my lunch.

TERESA: Drink your tea mother.

MARLEY: I heard you like the orient, so I found some exotic leaves. Oolong, Darjeeling.

IRENE: And just when are you planning this, this adventure.

TERESA: We had our second appointment last week.

IRENE: Appointment?

TERESA: For insemination.

IRENE: How dare you speak to me like that. Is this your idea of revenge?

MARLEY: We're excited. We thought you'd be happy.

IRENE: Since when do you care about my happiness. Honestly, I stop by with a peace offering, an olive plant, and what do I get? The pits.

MARLEY: I love olives.

IRENE: It's a metaphor.

MARLEY: I don't understand.

IRENE: A figure of speech.

TERESA: She knows what a metaphor is.

IRENE: It's just ornamental. It's not supposed to bear fruit.

TERESA: Ever since I can remember you've been carping about grandchildren.

IRENE: That's when I thought you'd marry someone with a penis.

MARLEY: We try not to use the "P" word.

TERESA: Wasn't that your main objection? That the purpose of marriage is procreation?

IRENE: This is a nightmare. Now I know how Phyllis Schlafly feels. Two women can't raise a child. You can't even manage a proper garden.

TERESA: We're not asking your permission.

MARLEY: I like the garden.

IRENE: It's vulgar. It just isn't natural.

TERESA: I know, that's why it's so expensive.

MARLEY: I'm thinking of adding some herbs. Chamomile. Maybe tea.

IRENE: Don't get smart with me. A child needs a mother and a father.

TERESA: Remind me again, why did you never remarry?

IRENE: And look how you turned out.

MARLEY: Just great! And someday, she'll be a great mother. Just like you.

IRENE: Don't patronize, Marley. It's unbecoming.

An alarm bell DINGS.

MARLEY pops up and runs inside, off-stage.

IRENE: What's that.

TERESA: It's a pregnancy test.

IRENE: Very nice. Twist the knife.

TERESA: You should call first. Someday you'll learn.

> *MARLEY returns, brings the test, holds it out to TERESA.*

MARLEY: I can't look.

TERESA: I can't.

MARLEY: Let's look together?

IRENE: Oh for pity sake.

> *IRENE grabs the test.*
>
> *TERESA and MARLEY watch her.*
>
> *IRENE looks at the results, makes the sign of the cross.*
>
> *TERESA and MARLEY squeal and hug. They kiss.*
>
> *IRENE moves to the spot where the olive plant rests. She pokes her foot around in the soil.*

IRENE: This needs something. To adjust the acid level.

End of Play

OUT OF INK 2006: Cricket Radio

Ingredients:

1. The town of Piscacadawadaquaddywoggin, Maine.
2. A countdown.
3. Chirping crickets.

The ingredients were contributed by Sue Scott of A Prairie Home Companion, Jamie Smith-Cantara, (then theatre critic for the Austin-American Statesman), and Teresa Ferguson of Radio Without Borders.

This collection of ten 5-minute radio plays was performed live with Foley sound in the FronteraFest Long Fringe at the Blue Theater, 916 Springdale Rd. in Austin in January of 2006.

Playwrights: Allan Baker, Rebecca Beegle, Katherine Catmull, Elizabeth Cobbe, Christopher J. Krejci, Max Langert, Candyce Rusk, Priscilla Sample, Katherine Tanney, and Jason Tremblay

Directors: Ron Berry, Emily Fordyce, Ginger Morris, and Sharon Sparlin

Performers: Travis Dean, Odile Nicole Del Giudice, Gina Houston, Chris Loveless, Carra Martinez, Adriene Mishler, David Pagano, Jorge Sermini, and Jose Villarreal

Production Staff:
Stage Manager: Jason Hays
Foley Sound: Clark Gray, Michael Guidry
Recorded Sound:: Bryan Schneider

ScriptWorks staff (Austin Script Works then):
Artistic Director: C. Denby Swanson
Producing Director: Christina J. Moore
Member Representative: Robin Myrick

WAITING IS NOT MERELY EMPTY HOPING

Katherine Catmull
© 2006

CHARACTERS

VOICE OFFSTAGE
A
B
HOSTESS

The waiting area of a very noisy restaurant. Besides the typical voices and clanging of doors and dishes, an occasional disturbingly inappropriate sound arises. Inappropriate sounds might include: a cat meowing to get out, strong wind in tall pines, a truck backing up, fragments of some odd pop song like the Kingston Trio's MTA Song, children chanting a poem; etc.

This background sound mass should be fairly thickly layered, begin as fairly normal, and get stranger as the piece progresses. Some sounds need to happen at specific times, whether by actor or sound person, and these are identified as "OFF" in the text. Probably most of these sounds seem to come from the next room, but some might come from nearby.

Although stage direction at end refers to A as "herself," A&B can be whatever gender works in the casting. A&B have to shout a bit, especially at first.

VOICE OFF: (*scream of laughter*)

A: The food's supposed to be incredible.

B: Yes, you said.

A: No, but I mean really — *so* worth trying.

B: Worth the *wait*.

A: Well yes. Sorry about that, I just didn't realize —

B: You didn't realize anyone but you reads the New York Times restaurant reviews.

A: No, of course, I mean I just didn't think that the very first night —

B: You didn't realize you live in a city with eight million other people; you thought you still lived in Piscacadawadaquaddywoggin, Maine.

A: Come on, you know how to pronounce it.

VOICE OFF: (*insistent*) I don't think you get what I'm *saying*, that's not what I'm *saying*, listen —

B: Miss, ma'am? Excuse me, sorry, miss? Yes. Where are we on the list now?

HOSTESS: Ah, oh yes, let me see — tenth.

B: Christ. We are never going to get a table. Why don't they take reservations again?

A: They think reservations are misleading.

B: They think — what?

A: They say reservations mislead you into believing that you have a certain…kind of control. That you don't actually have. I think. I wasn't sure I got that part.

B: Don't believe it. Reservations give you magic powers my friend. Reservations allow you to predict the future. Like: when you are going to eat.

A: I think it's part of their whole philosophy. There's no set menu, right? They just cook with whatever food is perfectly ripe that day. And so, same thing with the customers, see? whoever's here, whoever's *ripe* for *this* meal at *this* restaurant at *this* moment — it's almost sort of Zen, because —

VOICE OFF: (*terrible sobs in the background*)

Pause.

A: Anyway.

B: Miss? How many ahead of us — ?

HOSTESS: Still nine.

VOICE OFF: (*insistent*) I do want to, though, I do want to! I do want to, I do! I do want to (*fade off*)

B: How long have we been here? It seems like hours, it seems like days, I can't remember my former life …

A: Are you a little blood sugary, maybe? Because we can't have been here that long.

B: You don't remember either, do you?

VOICE OFF: *(cell phone loudness, hard edge)* Yeah I don't mean to be difficult, but I just don't see it that way. Right, I don't mean to be difficult, but I just don't see it that way. I see what you're saying... *(fade out)*

B: Bedlam. This place is Bedlam.

A: Bedlam is a contraction of Bethlehem.

B: What?

A: The place where Jesus was born. Bedlam. Is short for.

SOUND OFF: Cow lows softly

B: What the hell are you Oh say Miss? Where are we — where are we on the list?

HOSTESS: Still ninth, my goodness. Oh, no, wait: 8th.

VOICE OFF: Oh my GOD that smell, I will be SICK.

A: Are people actually eating in there? This place is maybe a little creepy after all. Do you want to go?

B: Do I want to GO? Now that we're EIGHTH, are you MAD? We're going to have dinner here or die. OR DIE.

A: You don't have to be mad at me about it.

SOUND OFF: ice cream truck playing Für Elise.

B: I just got shivers. I feel like I'm inside a giant head. I think this is a surreal government experiment of some kind.

A: Well but why would the New York Times review a surreal government exp —

VOICE OFF: *(high keening wail of grief)*

B: How, where, sorry: what's your name, my angel? My one last hope? tell me your name.

HOSTESS: It doesn't matter, because there are still seven parties ahead of you. No, six now: oh wait, five — four. Three parties ahead of you.

B: *(calling after her)* Are they parties though? Are they really parties in the truest sense? Because ours is not. Not so much a party.

A: You said you wanted to come.

B: I did want to come. Because you wanted to come. And I wanted to be nice to you so that I wouldn't feel so bad about how much I am starting to dread every moment of your endless goddamn chipper conversation.

                         Beat.

A: What? I didn't hear most of that. Are you mad?

                      The restaurant noise subsides a bit.

VOICE OFF: *(ecstatic, weeping laughter)*

A: Oooh the hostess is holding up three fingers over there, we must be third now.

B: We live here now, by the way. We live inside this collection of screams and sounds. I give into that now, the way you give into freezing.

HOSTESS: (*softly*) Two.

B: What happened? What did she say? Did she say two?

A: She said —

B: What's odd is that I am not at all hungry anymore. I think I must have already eaten.

A: Well I'm starv —

B: The noise fed me. I treasure the noise. But wait; where did it go?

>   *Gradually the noise has faded away. In the silence, we hear only the chirping of crickets.*

A: (*informatively*) Well, there's still crickets. Which is a little odd, actually. But you know, crickets are good luck in Asia, not just in China but in India too for example, so maybe they —

B: Quiet. Shhhh. Look, there she is: our angel.

A: She's actually been a bit *rude,* in my —

B: Shhh, shh. She's pointing at us.

A: She's pointing at YOU.

HOSTESS: (*beautifully*) One.

Crickets stop. Wind arises.

B: One. (*whispers*) One, one, one.

A: Where did you go? (*louder*) Are you there?

Silence.

This isn't as cool as I thought. No wait, I'm coming. Am I? Is there room for me?

Pause.

(*to herself*) Shhhhh.

End of Play

OUT OF INK 2007: Hybrid

Ingredients:

1. A hybrid.
2. Leaves.
3. A sudden reversal.

Ingredients were created by ScriptWorks in collaboration with David Nuñez of Dorkbot-Austin in an event for both SW member writers and electronic artists and makers.

The original production ran March 22-24 and 29-31, 2007 at The Blue Theater, 916 Springdale Rd. in Austin with the following company:

Playwrights: Rebecca Beegle, Katherine Catmull, Elizabeth Cobbe, Marc Frost, Aimée Gonzalez, Zack Gonzales, Max Langert, and P. Paullette MacDougal

Directors: Lowell Bartholomee, Emily Fordyce, Ellie McBride, Christina J. Moore, and Julia M. Smith

Performers: Kimberly Barrow, Tom Coiner, David DuBose, Carrie Fountain, Jude Hickey, Margaret Hoard, Rhonda Kulhanek, Nicole Marosis, Cara Martinez Noah Neal, and Robin Grace Thompson

Designers: Lowell Bartholomee (video), Pam Friday (costumes), Natalie George (lights), Marco Noyola (sets/props), and Skipper Chong Warson (sound)

Fight Choreography:
Travis Dean

Production Staff:
Stage Manager: Kate Kampschroeder

Deck Crew: Chris Kautz, Steven Laing
Electrician/Light Board Operator:
Austin Sheffield
Sound/Video Operator: Shawn Ferrell

ScriptWorks Staff (then Austin Script Works):
Artistic Director: C. Denby Swanson
Producing Director: Christina J. Moore
Member Representative: Aimée Gonzalez

AMERICAN WOMEN AND THEIR HATCHETS

Carrie Nation & Lizzie Borden
(A Re-Creation of Their Famed Vaudeville Act)
Rebecca Beegle
© 2006

BACKDROP

Black-and-white projection of the historical CN and LB, large and side-by-side.

ANNOUNCEMENT:
    Ladies And Gentlemen! American Women And Their Hatchets. Starring Lizzie Borden And Carrie Nation.

The two women begin in a linked-arm vignette. Each holds a hatchet made of molded flesh. The women share a long braid of hair between them, head to head, that they unravel and recoil as their act is performed.

BORDEN: Right away let me say I didn't do it.

NATION: I done every damn thing they said I done.

BORDEN: I loved my mother. She died when I was a child and left me alone.

NATION: I married an alcoholic.

BORDEN: With my father and his wife.

NATION: Dirty stinkin.

BORDEN: His *wife*.

NATION: Good for jack-all, smoke-in-a-hole, fool-for-nothin, damnable jack-robin of a two-cents worth a spit and shoeshine, talkin through his moth-eaten hat, lack of talent, drunker 'n a doughnut, soul-stealing, sewer-sucking, hem-ripping, chest-cleavin ripe-ass bastard man. Stone-footed. Tar-hearted. Left him right quick.

BORDEN: Everybody leaves. That's something I learned early. And I keep learning it. For instance, you will leave. Every last one of you.

NATION: I went after the enemy drink. For the rest of my life. Men, I have come to save you from a drunkard's fate.

BORDEN: I was a lady, an orphan, a spinster. But you all, you already know what they say about me.

NATION: They call me the Bar-Room Smasher!

BORDEN: Lizzie Borden took an axe
And gave her mother forty whacks
When she saw what she had done
She gave her father _____

NATION: You know how it goes.

BORDEN: How I hate that song. She wasn't my mother. My mother died when I was two. If she had lived. I would never raise a hand to my mother. If she had lived. She would have taught me to be sweet and gentle, and to fold my handkerchiefs so their lace corners kiss, and to brush out my dark hair one hundred times a night so in the morning it lay straight and shiny like the edge of a clean blade.

NATION: Living peaceful will only get you so far.

BORDEN: I believe in God. But not in family. Not anymore.

NATION: Liquor is the devil's blood and yet some folks willingly drink it. For pleasure!

BORDEN: I no longer believe in being related to anyone and I don't like being this close to you.

NATION: We're on the same side. We're on a mission. To shut the mouths of those rum-soaked, whiskey-swilled, saturn-faced rummies.

BORDEN: I did shut their mouths. I did. But still they talk. You know what they say? They say, she did it. And they look at me. And their look says, she did it. The way you are looking at me now. Here. Let us perform for you.

The women perform a choreographed waltz. LIZZIE BORDEN makes a deep bow, then:

BORDEN: I cleared my name in court but nowhere else.

NATION: I *made* my name. One morning I heard a voice, you see? Said: "Take something in your hands, and throw at these saloons, and smash them." The voice said, "I will stand by you." I took a hatchet, a sweet little axe, wide at one end and tight in the middle.

BORDEN: I do like knives.

NATION: And I smashed taverns, wherever and whenever I could, all across our great nation. So I took

	that as my surname. Nation, take a look at yourself.
BORDEN:	I like sharp things, with a handle to hold. But doesn't everyone?
NATION:	I conducted my Hatchetations alone or with a band of ladies. Ladies who understood as I did, deep in my seein' soul, that whiskey rots families from the inside out. I am a bulldog runnin along at the feet of Jesus, barking at what he doesn't like.
BORDEN:	I'm not what killed us. He did it. He who stood in the corner, pointing his finger like a loaded gun.
NATION:	When I'm a bulldog, I'm male. Otherwise, I'm a woman.
BORDEN:	Pointing at me. Lizzie Borden took an _____ And gave her mother forty _____ When she saw what she had _____ She gave her father _____
NATION:	"Good morning, destroyer of men's souls." That was my greeting to the barkeeps. Followed by, smash.

The hatchets emit a pulsing thump.

BORDEN:	I had a lot of money. Lot of good it did.
NATION:	I was a large woman. Six foot in my stocking feet and well round in the middle. Did a lot of good. Once scared a prizefighter right out of a tavern. Whiskey still burnin his lips.

BORDEN: Yes. Sharp. A nice narrow wooden handle. Something my small hands can master.

NATION: I live in Texas. We do these sorts of thing.

BORDEN: I didn't do it. But if I did do it, if I had done it.

NATION: No no no no no no darlin — don't change your story now.

BORDEN: I'm only saying, I would have had good reason to —

NATION: Now just shush shut up and stop talkin right now.

BORDEN: And the strength to —

NATION: Ah.Ah.Ah.

BORDEN: If I could go back, right now, to that parlor.

NATION: Forward only. Can only march forward.

BORDEN: That parlor smelled like another woman's powder, sickly sweet.

NATION: Hup two three four.

BORDEN: It filled my nose, clouded my brain.

NATION: Smash, ladies, smash!

BORDEN: Just for a moment, and then I saw clear.

The hatchets emit two pulsing thumps.

BORDEN: And I knew what I was.

NATION & BORDEN:
    Lizzie Borden _____
    And gave her _____
    When she saw_____
    She gave her _____ forty-one.

Pulsing thumps, first like a fast heartbeat, then slowing to a stop.

BORDEN: Everybody leaves.

NATION: Don't drink it. It will burn your lips. And rot you from the inside.

BORDEN: Learn early.

NATION: A bad marriage started my life, which I lived out strong and lark-happy. I made a difference.

BORDEN: Everybody leaves.

NATION: Smash, ladies.

BORDEN: I made a difference.

NATION: I made a difference.

BORDEN: I made a difference.

NATION: I made a difference.

BORDEN: I made a difference.

NATION: I made a difference.

BORDEN: I made a difference.

NATION: I made a difference.

> *The women salute us with the hatchets. Then the axe blades come off the hatchets and a mass of red sparks burst out of their tops, like the 4th of July. The women hold the handles aloft, higher and higher, as the sparks bleed out.*

End of Play

OUT OF INK 2008: Key Changes

Ingredients:

1. A character with a secret they are trying to hide.
2. A piece of music, some of which may have been forgotten.
3. A radical physical transformation (be it of person, place, or thing).

The ingredients were contributed by playwright/director/performer Daniel Alexander Jones, actor and director Jenny Larson, and Megan Monaghan, (then Literary Manager at South Coast Rep).

The original production ran April 3-5 and 10-12, 2008 at the Blue Theatre, 916 Springdale Rd. in Austin with the following company:

Playwrights: Katherine Catmull, Vicki Caroline Cheatwood, Elizabeth Cobbe, Aimée Gonzalez, Meg Haley, Marshall Ryan Maresca, Sarah Saltwick, and Tom Sime

Directors: Emily Fordyce, T. J. Gonzales, Christina J. Moore, and Ginger Morris

Performers: Mick D'Arcy, Jamison Driskill, Gina Houston, Hannah Kenah, Alan Lester, Nicole Marosis, Kayla Newman, Andrew Varenhorst, Jose Villarreal, Zeb L. West, and Amanda Yilmaz

Designers: Pam Fletcher-Friday & Monica Pasut-Gibson (costumes), Rocky Hopson (sets/props), Bryan Schneider (sound), Andi Schultes (lights)

Production Staff:
    Stage Manager: Kate Kampschroeder

Sound Operator: Sam Kokajko
Light Board Operator: Kate Kampschroeder
Deck Crew: Rocky Hopson, Mick D'Arcy, Alan Lester

ScriptWorks Staff (then Austin Script Works):
Executive Artistic Director: Christina J. Moore
Member Representative: Aimée Gonzalez

FOR THE FOURTEENTH TIME
Vicki Caroline Cheatwood
© 2007

CHARACTERS

BLUE, *cowboy, 19ish*
TEXIE, *female, 30*
RAYFORD, *female, 18*
SMALL, *30s, TEXIE's husband*
JESUS CHRIST ON THE MORNING SHOW, V.O.
APOSTLES

Note: *Throughout the play, no matter how energized someone's speech becomes, even in the heat of passion or panic, no one bothers to get up from the table.*

> *O.S. DOOR SLAM. Lights Up on kitchen table lit by lanterns and candlelight. TEXIE, RAYFORD and SMALL sit, sipping hot coffee. BLUE enters, dust flying off his clothes and hair. The others cover their coffee mugs.*

TEXIE: Dang it, Blue. I just swept.

BLUE: Sorry, Texie. What's that in your cup?

RAYFORD: It's coffee, Blue. You want mine?

BLUE: Thanks.

> *This is no small sacrifice. Sadly, BLUE only has eyes for TEXIE.*

BLUE: Storm's turned. It's headed this away.

TEXIE: We rode out plenty of Category 4's in this house.

BLUE: It's a Category 18.

RAYFORD: *Eighteen?*

SMALL: Any rain in it?

BLUE: Funny.

SMALL: I seen rain. Once. When I was a baby. So 'course I don't remember it.

> *SMALL hunkers down over his coffee. BLUE looks at TEXIE. RAYFORD looks at TEXIE too, but more like she's gonna pry TEXIE's eyeballs out with her fingernails.*

BLUE: They're saying on the radio that this could be it. They're calling it an official "Coming," and saying it could be the actual end. *(to TEXIE)* This could be the end of things. One last chance.

SMALL: We need to get the livestock bedded down and bolted in, and bury them gas cans so they don't go off in the storm, and carry the rest of the food down to the shelter.

BLUE: *(to TEXIE)* I'll help you in the barn. If you want.

TEXIE: *(a decision)* …Yes.

SMALL: *(not moving)* Let's get a move-on.

RAYFORD: *(at TEXIE and BLUE)* Small. You don't see no problem with this?

SMALL: Huh.

Blackout.
Transition Music.

Immediate Lights Up on Scene 2.
Everybody's just as they were three seconds ago.

SMALL: Wasting valuable time, people.

BLUE: Figured y'all'd already be underground.

TEXIE: Never heard the alert.

BLUE: Where's your radio?

TEXIE: Rayford "fixed" it.

RAYFORD: It was broke already. We were having to crank it every other minute.

BLUE: I can work it over if you want me to, Texie.

SMALL: Category 18?

BLUE: Category 18. That's what they're saying.

SMALL: What was the one that killed all them people in town?

ALL: Category 5.

BLUE: Y'all get it bad out here?

RAYFORD: *They* freaked out and spent all day in the shelter. I didn't. I stayed on the porch and let it come. The wind was —

SMALL: Loud.

RAYFORD: Crackling. In my body, through my whole body, *hard*. The sky was around me and through me, electric, the color was —

TEXIE: Moldy. Brackish.

SMALL: Let's get moving.

BLUE: Everybody in town said, "Looks like the Fourteenth Coming of Christ."

RAYFORD: I remember The Thirteenth Coming.

TEXIE: *(Scoffs. To the men.)* She was barely ten months old.

RAYFORD: I guess you would know that, Texie, as you were and *are* so incredibly much older than me. By some twelve years. *(to BLUE)* …There was a song playing on the radio. (speaks the lyrics) "Sugar, sugar/Ah, honey-honey/You are my candy girl/You got me wantin' you …" *(forgetting the words)* Something-something-something… *(to BLUE)* "pour a little sugar on me, honey/pour a little sugar on me, honey." Something like that.

SMALL: You sure got a nice voice, Rayford.

RAYFORD: Thank you, Small.

BLUE: I just barely remember The Thirteenth Coming, and I was six years old at the time. Middle of the day, I guess on a Saturday because we's in town, shopping at the IGA. One of the Heavenly Host came up to me in the cereal aisle and offered me a stick of candy, but he looked just like Santa Claus and I was always scared to death of Santa Claus, so I just froze up. Mama said, "Be polite to the Heavenly Host or I'll taken the hide offa you." So I took the candy out of his "hand" — whatever they call them things they got — but I never did like the taste of peppermint, so I give it back to him. Mama grabbed holt of my arm so hard, felt like my fingers was gonna bust like sausages in a frying pan. The Heavenly Host guy chucked me under the chin and smiled. And then he took in this great big breath of fire and sucked up Mama and blew her down into the pit of Hell, and then went on his way. That was something to see.

SMALL: We need to mobilize.

RAYFORD: Our Mama was lifted up, but Daddy was took to Hell. Texie never says why. *She* was plenty old at the time. She remembers, but she won't say. She don't realize that there's a *lot* that I remember, things I heard and things that I *know. A. Lot. Of. Things.*

TEXIE: I can't imagine nothing worse than The Thirteenth Coming. Breath of God blew through and drove the chickens halfway through the barn wall, beaks embedded in the tin. We lost nearly every animal on this place.

RAYFORD: And Mama was Raptured, her poor sick body lifted up by the Heavenly Host. Somebody took pictures of it as happened. Nobody got pictures of what happened to Daddy.

TEXIE: I don't know that I got that barn door shut good.

BLUE: Better go check it.

RAYFORD: Jesus, Small. Do something.

SMALL: Let's go, people. Get moving.

TEXIE: *(to BLUE)* Moving. Yes.

Blackout.
Transition Music.

Immediate Lights Up on Scene 3.
Again, everyone and everything are exactly the same

SMALL: Time's wasting. Sooner the better.

RAYFORD: The Thirteenth Coming wasn't near as bad as the Twelfth — and The Twelfth Coming wasn't as bad as the Eleventh, and so on and so on. You ever wonder why? If the Second Coming was the "end of the world" and there's been at least eleven more recorded "Comings," and eleven confirmed visits from the Christ Incarnate — and yet we're still not wiped out, people are still on this Earth — doesn't that make you wonder just how "all mighty powerful" God really is?

BLUE: Naw.

TEXIE: No.

SMALL: Nope.

BLUE: I'd sure like to have a crack at that radio, Texie.

TEXIE: You'll need a screwdriver from the tool room. In the barn.

> *Exasperated sigh from RAYFORD.*
>
> *Blackout.*
> *Transition Music.*
>
> *Immediate Lights Up on Scene 4.*
> *Again, no change on stage.*

BLUE: *(to TEXIE)* Got any more coffee?

TEXIE: Sure don't. Squeezed last cup of water outta the cistern this morning for bath day. It'll take a few weeks to get it back up to a foot deep.

BLUE: Y'all are lucky to have a deep well. We recycle our own piss, but it's damn hard to work up a piss when you ain't had nothing but a half-cup of piss every 34½ hours.

SMALL: I miss spittin'. Man, I used to love to spit. We all got to make some changes.

RAYFORD: *(to BLUE)* Take me to the barn. I'll put soft butter in my mouth.

BLUE: *(to TEXIE)* You got butter?

> *Blackout.*

Transition Music.

Immediate Lights Up on Scene 5. Nothing's changed with the people. STATIC, VOICES, DISTANT MUSIC comes from the radio.

SMALL: Where'd they say that storm was?

BLUE: Around down Livingston.

TEXIE: Guess it's time.

RAYFORD: I'm not going down there.

TEXIE: Category *18*, Rayford. Don't be an idiot.

RAYFORD: *(to BLUE)* Considering my suspect origins, it is a miracle that I am not an idiot.

TEXIE: *(to RAYFORD)* If I have to, I will drag you and your filthy mind down into that shelter.

RAYFORD: Because you made a promise. To Mama.

TEXIE: Yes, I did.

RAYFORD: What about the promise to the Lord? The one that goes "Clinging ye only unto *him*." *(pointing at SMALL)*

SMALL: Time to get a move on, people.

TEXIE: Get downstairs, Rayford. Now.

RAYFORD: Y'all go on down, all three of you, and I'll be right here waiting, so that when Jesus comes, I can relate to him about what-all commandments been busted around here tonight.

BLUE: I better git.

TEXIE: No.

SMALL: Dust is blowing awful thick.

TEXIE: You should spend the night.

TEXIE & RAYFORD: In the barn.

If the eye contact between TEXIE and BLUE were suddenly manifested into the physical realm, it'd be porn.

RAYFORD: Oh good God.

SMALL: We all gotta pitch in.

RAYFORD: Small. I pray you are not a man who lives up to his name.

SMALL: Huh?

RAYFORD: Take me downstairs. Now.

Blackout.
Transition Music.
FOUR EXPLOSIONS, each deeper and bigger than the last, until the fourth one vibrates the seats.

Lights Rise to half. SMALL and BLUE are the only ones left on stage. There's a full pot of coffee on the table. The women are gone. SOUND: BIRDSONG, loud. Static clears and a gorgeous male voice comes over the radio.

JESUS: *(V.O.)* Good morning, good people. This is Jesus Christ in the Morning.

APOSTLES: And we're the Apostles!

Throughout, The APOSTLES punch up Jesus' remarks with sycophantic laughter and inane commentary.

JESUS: *(V.O.)* In case you slept through it last night [*laughter*], that *was* an official "Coming". I mean, I'm here. I came. [*apostles' laughter*] We're gonna open the phone lines in a minute to take your questions about what The Fourteenth Coming accomplished, why are those of you still here — well, why *are* you here and not Raptured or otherwise dispatched, and will the Earth ever see rain again? We'll do our best to answer these and all your questions. Be right back, I promise.

SOUND: insipid "oldie" — maybe "Sugar, Sugar."

BLUE: Jesus God. Who's idea of paradise is this?

Beat. They drink coffee.

SMALL: I know where she kept it.

BLUE: What?

SMALL: The butter.

BLUE: Ah. Shit.

Blackout.

End of Play

OUT OF INK 2009: Time Steps

Ingredients:

1. The play must move backward, from end to beginning.
2. The play must include a dance break which causes a shift in the action.
3. The play must include three things your mother told you not to do.

The ingredients were contributed by Michael John Garces, Artistic Director of Cornerstone Theatre in Los Angeles, Natalie George, lighting designer, and director, Emily Fordyce.

The original production ran March 26-28 and April 2-4, 2009 at the Blue Theatre, 916 Springdale Rd. in Austin with the following company:

Playwrights: Katherine Catmull, Aimée Gonzalez, Meg Haley, Max Langert, Marshall Ryan Maresca, Susan McMath Platt, Sarah Saltwick, and Timothy Thomas

Directors: TJ Gonzales, Heather Huggins, Ellie McBride, Christina J. Moore

Performers: Kelli Bland, Kenneth Wayne Bradley, David DuBose, Kathleen Fletcher, David Gallagher, Anne Hulsman, Michelle Keffer, Rhonda Kulhanek, Christopher Loveless, Nicole Marosis, and Zeb L. West

Designers: Olivia Biggs (set/props), Pam Friday (costumes), Natalie George (lights), and Bryan Schneider (sound)

Production Staff:
    Production Manager: Dani Pruitt

Stage Manager: Kate Kampschroeder
Asst. Stage Manager: Elijah Gray
Light Board Operator: Shawn Ferrell
Sound Operator: Bryan Schneider
Deck Crew: Elijah Gray, Cailean Bilsky

ScriptWorks Staff:
Executive Artistic Director: Christina J. Moore
Member Representative: Aimée Gonzalez

COWBOY FANTASIA
Sarah Saltwick
© 2008

CHARACTERS

JOLENE
CLINT
YOUNGER JOLENE
YOUNGER CLINT

JOLENE, a tired looking country princess, sits on the floor, too close to the television. She is eating mashed potatoes.

CLINT, a cowboy, enters.

CLINT: What happened to the clocks, Jo?

JOLENE: I don't know what you're talkin' about, Clint.

CLINT: I'm talkin' about the front porch. I'm talkin' about the back porch. I'm talkin' about the steps and I'm talkin' about the clocks, gears and them little wires.

JOLENE: Don't yell indoors.

CLINT: Don't you sit so close to the tv. Turn it off. We're talkin'.

JOLENE: Don't you "don't" me.

She turns it off.

CLINT: What happened to the clocks, Jolene?

JOLENE: I didn't wanna to know what time it was.

Pause. He considers this.

CLINT: You're crazy.

JOLENE: You like it.

CLINT: I didn't say I didn't.

JOLENE: You like it when I'm —

CLINT: I like you almost all the time. You wanna to fight about this —

JOLENE: I just didn't wanna to know the time anymore —

CLINT: I'll fight about this —

JOLENE: I already feel old, I feel so old —

CLINT: I'd rather not fight — you're not old — that's what got you? That's your boogieman?

JOLENE: I feel different.

CLINT: Girl —

JOLENE: Woman —

CLINT: You're what you always was. Don't you forget. I see you. I've never looked away. You? You've been looking away from me?

She shakes her head. He embraces her and dips her into a deep kiss. It is aggressive, possessive and hot.

SCENE FOUR
They are fighting.

CLINT: That ain't no lipstick.

JOLENE: I know lipstick. I know my color and I don't know this!

CLINT: You're makin' up things.

JOLENE: You been late all this week.

CLINT: Cows don't know about clocks.

JOLENE: What about other houses? What about hotel rooms? They won't tell you what time it is? She ain't got the decency to tell you it's late and you best get? If I was steppin' out, I'd have the good sense to keep my watch on.

CLINT: You done?

JOLENE: You done?

CLINT: I ain't gonna sit here and remind you what love is.

JOLENE: So you're leavin'? You're walkin' out?

CLINT: No.

JOLENE: So you're stayin'?

CLINT: You're different, Jolene.

JOLENE: I ain't. You're looking at me different, that's all.

CLINT: Maybe.

JOLENE: So what now?

CLINT: We wait.

JOLENE: For what?

CLINT: For each to look right. Familiar.

They look at each other.

JOLENE: This might take some time.

SCENE THREE

They are kissing.

CLINT: You going to kiss me like that when we're old and argue 'bout bills?

JOLENE: You're jumping ahead a things.

CLINT: I like to know where I'm going.

JOLENE: I'd like to know where you've been.

CLINT: You've been looking at me long enough to know.

JOLENE: You think you're the only cowboy I dance with?

CLINT: Dying breed.

JOLENE: Still got some life. Shoot, it's late.

CLINT: It ain't late, it's early.

JOLENE: Not what that clock says.

CLINT: That one's a liar. You been married?

JOLENE: Not yet. You been?

CLINT: Sure.

JOLENE: Shoot. It's late and you're sayin' things I ought know.

CLINT: Just a few times.

JOLENE: How many's a few? More than twice? Three? Four? One whole hands worth?

He nods and shrugs.

CLINT: I like parties and girls in white dresses. Church. Preachers.

JOLENE: Easter's every year.

CLINT: You think about it? Trying that dress on?

JOLENE: I like my jeans just fine.

CLINT: You think about forever havin' one face?

JOLENE: That's way you look at it? No wonder you're getting it wrong.

CLINT: How do you look at it?

JOLENE: People change.

CLINT: I know.

JOLENE: You got to expect it. Like it maybe even.

CLINT: You don't dance like no philosopher.

JOLENE: How many you dance with?

CLINT: That is a personal question.

JOLENE: You still got more in that heart of yours? You're telling me, you got some five ex-wives out there, five ladies cursin' you as they brush their teeth, you got five days of the year — maybe more — when you know someone out there is lying 'bout why they're crying? — you got all that, and you're biting for more?

> *DANCE SEQUENCE: JOLENE by Dolly Parton plays loud. They dance. They dance as lovers, comfortable and bold with each. Two other actors a young man and a young woman enter. They cut in and the four dance. The older pair leave the floor and the new couple is left dancing together, awkward but hopeful - strangers.*

SCENE TWO

YOUNGER CLINT: You been here before? —

YOUNGER JOLENE: (*interrupting*) You been here before? —

YOUNGER CLINT: I come here. End of the week. Most weeks.

YOUNGER JOLENE: Look at the girls?

YOUNGER CLINT: Listen to the music. I always play that song, that Jolene song. It just finished.

YOUNGER JOLENE: I heard it.

> *Pause. He is pleased, though not surprised. He keeps hold of her.*

YOUNGER JOLENE: You love that song?

YOUNGER CLINT: The music.

YOUNGER JOLENE: Not the words?

YOUNGER CLINT: The words get me nervous.

YOUNGER JOLENE: Why, you looking for trouble, cowboy?

YOUNGER CLINT: No ma'am.

YOUNGER JOLENE: Guess what?

YOUNGER CLINT: What?

YOUNGER JOLENE: That ain't no guess.

YOUNGER CLINT: Give me a hint then.

YOUNGER JOLENE: What's your name?

YOUNGER CLINT: Clint. What's yours?

YOUNGER JOLENE: Guess.

YOUNGER CLINT: (*slowly*) Jolene.

YOUNGER JOLENE: You're smarter than you look. So we're still dancing…

YOUNGER CLINT: Seem to be.

YOUNGER JOLENE: I said I'd give you one dance.

YOUNGER CLINT: Well, I'll steal this one and we'll split the bill on the next.

YOUNGER JOLENE: You flirt like a married man.

YOUNGER CLINT: You flirt like a country song.

YOUNGER JOLENE: That don't make a lick of sense. Why are you after me?

YOUNGER CLINT: I like your face.

SCENE ONE

Earlier that night, in the bar. They are each alone, checking each other out on the sly.

YOUNGER JOLENE: (*to her friends*). You go talk to him. He might be lookin' at you too, who knows? What am I going to do with a cowboy? Some wannabe rancher oilman. Didn't his mama tell him to be a doctor or lawyer or such? What do you do with an open-air man used to ridin' off into the sitting down sun? Used to branding his babes with a hot iron poker without some much as a thank you?

He approaches her.

YOUNGER CLINT: You looking at me? I can come little closer.

YOUNGER JOLENE: You're standing under the t.v.

YOUNGER CLINT: You dance?

YOUNGER JOLENE: Not with strangers. Mama raised me right.

YOUNGER CLINT: I bet.

He starts to leave.

YOUNGER JOLENE: Do you?

YOUNGER CLINT: I don't believe in strangers.

YOUNGER JOLENE: Is that some sort of a cowboy thing?

YOUNGER CLINT: You wanna dance with me? I wanna dance to this song comin' up — this next song. I bet you'd like it. I bet it's your kind of music. You wanna dance with me?

YOUNGER JOLENE: That's all you're after?

He doesn't answer.

YOUNGER JOLENE: I'll give you one song. I ain't given you anything more. So don't ask.

YOUNGER CLINT: I won't ask.

YOUNGER JOLENE: One song. I'll know when it's over. Don't think I won't stop. I'll know when it ends.

He takes her hands, moving her towards him.

JOLENE begins to play….

End of Play

OUT OF INK 2010: The Trunk Show

Ingredients:

1. Write a "Trunk Show." In other words, the contents of the physical world of the play must be contained in or represented by a trunk or several trunks…or an elephant trunk, or a tree trunk…
2. The play must include these four actions:
   something must be sold;
   something must be traded;
   something must be given;
   something must be refused;
3. The play must contain a "healer."

The ingredients were contributed by playwright and former ScriptWorks Artistic Director, John Walch, actor and educator, Babs George, and Todd London, (then Artistic Director of New Dramatists).

The original production ran May 13-15 and 20-22, 2010 at the Blue Theatre, 916 Springdale Rd. in Austin with the following company:

Playwrights: Allison Orr Block, Katherine Catmull, Vicki Caroline Cheatwood, Elizabeth Cobbe, Trey Deason, Meg Haley, Susan McMath Platt, C. Denby Swanson

Dramaturg: Kristin Harrison

Directors: Lowell Bartholomee, Ellie McBride, Christina J. Moore, Sharon Sparlin

Performers: Monika Bustamante, Mick D'Arcy, David DuBose, Anne Hulsman, Michelle Keffer, Christopher Loveless, John McNeill, Rebecca Robinson, Robin Grace Thompson, Jacob Trussell

Designers: Pam Friday (costumes), Natalie George (lights), Johnny Gonzales (set/props), Bryan Schneider (sound)

Production Staff:

Producer's Assistant:	Dani Pruitt
Stage Manager:	Taylor Kulhanek
Asst. Stage Manager:	Elijah Gray
Light Board Operator:	Bernard Klinke
Sound Operator:	Dax Taruc
Deck Crew:	Elijah Gray, Kyle Houseworth

ScriptWorks Staff:

Executive Artistic Director:	Christina J. Moore
Member Representative:	Aimée Gonzalez

WHAT HAVE YOU GOT TO LOSE?
Katherine Catmull
© 2009

CHARACTERS

GUY
WOMAN

Empty stage. A GUY walks out. Not exactly homeless looking but getting there. He talks to the audience, crying his wares.

GUY: What have you got to lose?

What have you got to lose?

Stomach ulcers. Ovarian cysts. Might-be-cancers. Lumps of old pain. What have you got to lose? *(Pause.)*

Tough crowd.

Tough, but not too tough for me. I can work my way in. *(Holds up his hands.)* Magic fingers. You won't even have to put in a quarter. I promise. I can pull it out. I can pull it all out. All the things you don't want. Pain. Disease. Shit. Fat.

Look at me. I've done it to myself. I've taken out everything that caused me any pain. Inside, now, I'm just a network of clean, blood-red rivers and tributary creeks. And a small, glistening stomach, ready to wring dry the few bites of food that are all I need.

I am light inside. Squeaky clean. My blood is clear as red crystal.

I'll still grow old, sure. But I will not age — I will condense. I'll wither like a healthy apple, getter darker and rosier, with a sweeter, deeper scent. My skin will pucker over the emptiness, settle into itself.

Sound good? Of course, it sounds good. And I could do the same for you. I can take all the bad stuff away, leave you clean as a flute.

What have you got to lose?

> *A WOMAN steps out of the audience, uncertain, nervous, maybe playing it a little for a joke.*

WOMAN: I don't even know if this is real.

GUY: That's right.

WOMAN: Okay so but I'll play along. *(Small laugh. Glances around.)* So you can take out fat?

GUY: Yes.

WOMAN: I feel fat sometimes.

GUY: Uh huh.

WOMAN: Are you saying I look fat?

> *He shrugs.*

WOMAN: Uh, so, well. *(Laughs.)* Would you — can you?

GUY: Yes. If that's all you want. If that's as far as your imagination extends.

WOMAN: What do you mean?

GUY: Nothing else in there you'd like to get rid of? Something deeper? Something truer? No lumps of old pain, for example?

WOMAN: Well —

GUY: Congealed hurt? Rotting offense? Shards of heartbreak?

She looks at him, confused.

GUY: Because you look sad to me. And here's the thing — I could take all that away. It would all be gone. Every ugly word anyone ever said to you. Every death. Every slap. Nothing to haunt you at 3am except what you left off the grocery list.

WOMAN: You can do that?

GUY: You interested.

WOMAN: I might be. I might be! Wow. Could you really do that?

GUY: Maybe. What have you got for me?

WOMAN: Um, I already paid to get in here.

GUY: Really, you did? Because most of these people were comped. (*Beat.*) But it doesn't matter. Paying just gets you in. It doesn't get anything out.

WOMAN: Well — okay, how much —

GUY: "Money." Do I look like I charge money? No. Trade. Fair trade. Like the coffee.

WOMAN: I don't have anything to trade with you.

GUY: I'll be the judge of that. Lie down.

WOMAN: Do you need me to — to — (*touches clothes, glances at audience*)

GUY: If I can push through skin, I can push through whatever you can get at the Gap. Magic fingers.

> *She lies down and closes her eyes. He drapes something over her — a scarf or jacket, some garment he was wearing — that obscures what he is doing to her torso. He pulls out an old wooden toy.*

GUY: What's that?

WOMAN: (*eyes still closed*) That's my cat that died the day before I left for college. We were the same age.

> *He pulls out a rain hat.*

WOMAN: We kissed in the rain. I was barefoot. He said he would call but he never did.

> *He pulls out a plastic jewel ring, a green jewel.*

WOMAN: My grandfather said I was stupid.

> *A worn prayer flag.*

WOMAN:	It was the best job I ever had. I don't know what I did wrong. They didn't even say.

He sits back.

GUY:	I'll take it. I'll take it all.
WOMAN:	(*Eyes open, she sits up.*) What do you mean?
GUY:	I'll take it off your hands. Or out of your tru —
WOMAN:	You mean — you'll take it out, and you'll keep it?
GUY:	Maybe. What difference does it make?
WOMAN:	Why would you keep it? Why would you want it?
GUY:	Because — look I have to want it, or it doesn't work, the magic doesn't —
WOMAN:	But why would you want it?
GUY:	Why do you CARE? Don't you want to get rid of all this old crap, all this old shit, all this old grief and trauma and —
WOMAN:	Stop it, don't. I've changed my mind. I don't want someone else to have my — Get away from me. Give me my — (*She begins to move away, reaches for the toy, hat, etc.*)
GUY:	(*pulling the stuff away, holding it*) Wait, don't. Stop. Don't, please, I need you. I need this. Please, I need your shit, I need your pain, I need your disease and wait, please, just stop, wait.

WOMAN: What is wrong with you?

GUY: I took mine out. I took it all out. I took out my heart. It was so full of old — old feeling, old pain, old joys that were turning into new pain. No heart! I didn't think what that would mean. There's nothing in there to pump the blood. My blood just hangs inside me, red and shiny, not moving. My blood just hangs there!

WOMAN: But you said you were light —

GUY: Yes, I'm light. I'm light as an empty box. I'm light as a pot hanging on the wall. I need something in me to cook, I didn't know, please. I'm so hungry.

WOMAN: Hungry for other people's tumors?

GUY: Tumors. Cysts. Fat. Warts. Pain. Grief. I am knitting them together. I am knitting up a heart, a new heart.

Please. You have plenty of pain. I don't have any. I'm so hungry.

He puts on the rain hat. He puts on the ring. A long pause.

WOMAN: Not the cat.

GUY: The cat was the most beautiful —

WOMAN: NOT THE CAT. The kiss, and the not calling. And my stupid grandfather, yes. You can have those. I'm not done with the firing yet, I'm still using it. And never, never the cat.

GUY: But it's not enough!

WOMAN: She was a little black cat. She was so dainty and polite. And when I picked up her body to bury her, it was the first time she ever felt heavy.

A pause.

GUY: All right. All right.

Another pause.

WOMAN: You're welcome.

She leaves.

GUY: (*to audience, still wearing rain hat and ring*) Anyone else? (*an attempt at his old manner*) What have you got to lose?

A long silence. He leaves. Blackout.

End of Play

OUT OF INK 2011: Forgetting Finnegan

Ingredients:

1. The dialogue must include passages from the end and the beginning of Finnegan's Wake by James Joyce.
2. The play must include a ceremony of forgetting.
3. Time is running out.

The ingredients were contributed by local actor and (then professor of theatre at St. Edward's University) Ev Lunning, Jr., scenic designer Leilah Stewart, and Gary Garrison, (then Executive Director of Creative Affairs for the Dramatists' Guild.)

The original production ran April 7-9 and 14-16, 2011 at Salvage Vanguard Theatre, 2803 Manor Rd. in Austin with the following company:

Playwrights: Lowell Bartholomee, Devo Carpenter, Amparo Garcia-Crow, Max Langert, Marshall Ryan Maresca, Susan McMath Platt, Sarah Saltwick, and Hank Schwemmer

Dramaturgs: Elizabeth Cobbe, Candyce Rusk

Directors: Debbie Lynn Carriger, Ellie McBride, Christina J. Moore, and Sharon Sparlin

Performers: Michelle Brandt, Victoria Eisele, Sharon Elmore, Rhonda Kulhanek, Christopher Loveless, Robert Pierson, Justin Scalise, Jacob Trussell, Jose Villarreal, and Zeb West

Designers: Pam Friday (costumes), Natalie George (lights), Johnny Gonzalez (sets/props), Bryan Schneider (sound)

Production Staff:
　　Stage Manager:　　　　Taylor Kulhanek
　　Asst. Stage Manager:　Josh "Bear" Singleton
　　Light Board Operator:　Taylor Kulhanek
　　Sound Board Operator:　Bryan Schneider
　　Deck Crew:　　　　　　Aaron Peña,
　　　　　　　　　　　　　Josh "Bear" Singleton

ScriptWorks Staff:
　　Executive Artistic Director:　Christina J. Moore
　　Member Representative:　　　Aimée Gonzalez

JOYCE, OR THE UNKNOWING
Hank Schwemmer
© 2011

For my mom

CHARACTERS

JAMES, *male, 50*
JOYCE, *female, 80*

JAMES: (*In darkness.*) And....

> *A deep, deep breath.*

> *LIGHTS UP on JOYCE in bed. JAMES holds her head in his hands, his own head less than two inches from hers. If it looks like a kiss, it's not. Most of a minute goes by. JAMES exhales, coughs and settles back, clearly winded by exertion. JOYCE opens her eyes, breathes. Pause.*

JOYCE: OK.

JAMES: OK? (*She nods.*) Senior prom. The band. Every song they played. The singer's patter in between songs. Your corsage. Drinking warm beer out behind the sawmill afterward. (*Slight pause. She nods.*) The Pieffer kid screaming by the back door, four stray dogs closing in on him. You and the mop handle. Bring him inside and give him some chocolate milk. In the…plastic cowboy boot cup.

JOYCE: The blue one. (*Nods.*)

JAMES: The smell of Absorbine Junior in the upstairs bathroom. (*Pause. She nods.*) The day Uncle Joe died. A Thursday. (*She nods.*) Your mom's in the hospital with Uncle Johnny. The neighbor lady watches the rest of you. She calls you "Suzy," the name you will respond to until you are 14. You are three.

JOYCE smiles, nods.

JAMES: November. The combines have been through the corn field. You and your family scavenge for leftover ears to take to the mill and feed to the steer. Oscar. Four bags.

JOYCE: OK, stop.

JAMES: There's a lot more.

JOYCE: I know.

She nods. JAMES takes her head in his hands.

JAMES: And….

He takes in a deep breath. Holds it as long as possible. He gasps and coughs upon exhaling. JOYCE opens her eyes. Slight pause.

JOYCE: OK.

JAMES: OK? Umm. "A way a lone a last a loved a long the…riverrun, past Eve and Adam's, from swerve of shore to bend of bay, …"

BOTH: "…brings us by a commodius vicus of recirculation …"

JAMES: "… back to Howth Castle and Environs."

JOYCE: (*Smiling.*) You do that a lot. You start at the end of the book and loop back to the first page.

JAMES: I'm sorry.

JOYCE: Can't you tell the beginning from the end?

JAMES: Look, can we …?

JOYCE: It's OK sweetheart. (*Pause.*)

JAMES: Your daughter runs away.

JOYCE: I remember.

JAMES: She spends the first night …

JOYCE: (*Firmly.*) I remember.

JAMES: …spends the first night behind the utility shed out at Green Lane park.

JOYCE glares at him, nods.

JAMES: (*Changing tack.*) Using the tip of your little finger, trying to adjust your hearing aids so they stop squealing.

JOYCE looks at him quizzically.

JAMES: Did this already.

JOYCE: Hearing aids?

JAMES: Used to squeal. We'd say, "Mom, you're feeding back." Got it?

JOYCE: I suppose. Hearing aids?

JAMES: Things are getting fuzzy, huh? (*She nods.*) That's gonna happen.

> *JAMES reaches for her head. She stops him.*

JOYCE: Now I remember. Hearing aids.

JAMES: We did this already.

JOYCE: I still remember. My early 40s, there was nerve damage. The flu.

JAMES: Should've told the doctor earlier.

JOYCE: Keep your shoulds to yourself. (*Pause.*) You were at the other end of the kitchen. I was cleaning up after supper. Pork chops, green beans and applesauce. I asked, "Are you planning to visit Mikey tonight?" And we talked a little about you borrowing the car and whether Mikey's truck was going to last the winter. And when I wasn't looking…a five-second gap came along in the conversation. And I said something else. And whatever I said just… hung there like a broken branch. You were gone. I couldn't hear you leave. A pit opened up inside me. (*With an edge.*) I won't miss that at all. Now.

JAMES: Do you remember what you said?

JOYCE: (*Firmly.*) Now.

> *JAMES holds her head, inhales, holds. When he exhales he is wracked by a coughing fit. JOYCE puts her arms around him, attempts to soothe him.*

JAMES: (*Still coughing.*) I'm OK. The peeling green paint …

JOYCE: Breathe. (*He does.*)

JAMES: The peeling green paint on the front porch swing. (*JOYCE nods.*) Dad volunteering to wash the dishes but always making one of us do the silverware. (*JOYCE nods.*) Uncle Ash playing guitar and getting all the cousins to sing "Cold, Cold Heart" at Christmas.

JOYCE: I barely remember that.

JAMES: You stopped going a long time ago. Look, time's running out.

JOYCE: AND DON'T SIT THERE TELLING ME TIME'S RUNNING OUT! I KNOW TIME'S RUNNING OUT! THAT'S THE ONLY THING TIME EVER DOES! (*Pause.*) What are you going to do with all this?

JAMES: I don't know. (*Pause.*)

JOYCE: Are you ready? (*He nods.*) Thank you.

JAMES: You're 29 years old…and you're in the hospital with…(*JAMES fights tears*)…

JOYCE: Thank you, James.

JAMES: … your first child. He will be named after his father. He will get straight A's from 1st through 5th grade. After age 9 he will never make his bed again. He will write letters home. He will live 2000 miles away. He will somehow convince you to read the complete works of James Joyce. He will…do what he can. He will do the remembering. And as long as…as long as he lives he…will never ….(*JAMES cannot continue.*)

JOYCE: I know.

JOYCE kisses his hands, puts one on her head and holds the other over her eyes. JAMES leans in close.

JOYCE: And …

JAMES takes a deep deep breath, held almost forever. He is once again wracked by the exhale. He pulls himself together.

JAMES: I'm going to take my hand away from your eyes now.

He does.

JAMES: Open your eyes.

She does.

JOYCE: "My leaves have drifted from me. All. But one clings still. I'll bear it on me."

JAMES: (*Pause.*) We've already done that. You're quoting *Finnegan's Wake*. We've already done that.

JOYCE: Looks like it won't leave. Must be important to me.

JAMES: (*Pause.*) Are you ready?

JOYCE nods, gets out of bed. JAMES escorts her to the door.

JOYCE: You seem very familiar.

JAMES smiles, if perhaps weakly.

JOYCE: Thank you.

JOYCE exits. The door closes. JAMES lays his hands on the door. JAMES moves back to the bed. Climbs in.

End of Play

OUT OF INK 2012: Sound Off

Ingredients:

1. Write a play with three hundred characters that takes place over 3000 years.
2. Include a children's song, game, or fairy tale.
3. Include a sound that everyone hears differently.

The ingredients were contributed by playwright Sibyl Kempson, playwright/director/poet Zell Miller, III, and playwright Suzan Zeder, (then Head of Playwriting at University of Texas).

The original production ran April 19-21 and 26-28, 2012 at the Blue Theatre, 916 Springdale Rd. in Austin, with the following company:

Playwrights: Bob Barr, Elizabeth Cobbe, Trey Deason, Amparo Garcia-Crow, Aimée Gonzalez, Marshall Ryan Maresca, Ann Maria Newsome (Wynter), and C. Denby Swanson

Dramaturg: Kristin Harrison

Directors: Lowell Bartholomee, Debbie Lynn Carriger, Ellie McBride, Jason Phelps, and Sharon Sparlin

Performers: Sarah Bading, Beth Burroughs, Amy Chang, David DuBose, Anna Maria Garcia, Heather Hanna, Anne Hulsman, Rhonda Kulhanek, Jenny Lavery, Christopher Loveless, Jason Phelps, and Aron Taylor

Designers: Robert Fisher (sound), Pam Fletcher-Friday (costumes), George Marsolek (sets/props), and Jennifer Rogers (lighting)

Production Staff:
    Asst. to Producer: Kayla Newman

Stage Manager: Cassandra Castillo
Asst. Stage Manager: Christina Smith
Sound Operator: TC Fletcher
Light Board Operator: Andrew Smith
Deck Crew: Dustin Miller

ScriptWorks Staff:
Executive Artistic Director: Christina J. Moore
Member Representative: Aimée Gonzalez

THE NORTH START TRANSGALACTIC INCIDENT

Anne Maria Newsome (Wynter)
©2011

CHARACTERS

PATRICIA, *an old woman*
ALEX, *a young man*
STATION, *an employee at North Star Transgalactic*
V/O *Shuttle, automated voice that gives shuttle instructions*
V/O CHARLENE, V/O YOUNG CHLOE, V/O ELDERLY CHLOE, V/O
PATRICIA'S SON, *voices from Earth*
LOVED ONES, *a chorus of almost 300 people*

PATRICIA and ALEX are in a space ship in a section of the ship that houses the control panel as well an observatory/lounge. The ship décor is similar to that of a hotel room. ALEX is dressed in uniform and sitting at the control panel. PATRICIA is dressed for comfort and reclining in a sort of lounge chair.

PATRICIA: Well, I think this is the best day we've had, hands down, Alex. The Earth has never looked this bright and clear.

ALEX: I'm glad you're enjoying it, Mrs. Lexington.

PATRICIA: If you don't start calling me Patricia you can forget about your gratuity. What's 15% of twenty million dollars?

ALEX: Three million, Mrs. Lexingt-, — Patricia. I'm going to sign us off now.

PATRICIA: Oh wait wait, I haven't called Chloe yet. She's the youngest of the brood …

ALEX: It must be nice having so many children and grandchildren.

PATRICIA: Most of them are just greedy mouths waiting for me to die. Well I'm still here, you bastards. Actually, let me just record a lullaby for the girl and you can send her parents the file.

> *ALEX starts the recording on his control panel and gives her the signal. PATRICIA sings.*

Twinkle Twinkle Little Star
How I wonder what you are
Up above the world so high
Like a grandma in the sky

(*laughing*) Oh, I just thought of that, just now! Quite funny! Good night, dear Madison — uh Chloe. Sleep tight. (*She cues ALEX to stop the recording.*) Can't keep them all straight for the life of me.

ALEX: This is Peterson signing off from Shuttle 82QP.

STATION: North Star Transgalactic Base Station, confirming your sign off. Mrs. Lexington, sweet celestial dreams from all of us at the base. And as always, thank you for traveling with us.

ALEX: I'll help you to your room.

PATRICIA: I would love to sleep here, actually.

ALEX: I'm sorry, but I'm not allowed to let you stay in the control room alone.

PATRICIA: I know you can lock that control board, I've seen you do it. There's no need to worry about me, I won't touch anything. I just like being in the front of the shuttle. I'm sure it's all in my head but I swear it feels different up here, like I'm charging toward unknown territories I just need a blanket over me and I'll be sleeping like, well, like an old woman with the world's worst jet lag.

ALEX: (*giving in*) Let me activate the shade so the sun won't keep waking you up.

He activates the shade.

I'll be back momentarily with your blanket.

He stands up and starts walking, then falls to the floor.

Shit! I'm sorry, Mrs. Lexington. The settings must be up a bit too high on the simulated gravity. I'll adjust them.

PATRICIA: Don't worry about the blanket. I'm cozy enough. Are you alright?

ALEX: I'll live.

PATRICIA: Sit down. You don't like being here do you?

ALEX: Of course I do.

PATRICIA: Tell the truth.

ALEX: The truth is this is a wonderful —

PATRICIA: Alex. Something's had you down since the beginning of the trip. I insist on knowing what is.

ALEX: Okay. I just — I hate simulated gravity. Don't you find it crazy that we would simulate something that holds us down and that eliminates one of the defining characteristics of space?

PATRICIA: I suppose —

ALEX: This isn't exactly what I'm trained to do.

PATRICIA: No?

ALEX: No! I'm sorry, no. I trained to be an astronaut. I'm a scientist and I've never worked on the space station. I haven't once been outside of the shuttle on EVA…there's not even a space suit on board.

PATRICIA: What if you need to go out there and fix something?

ALEX: North Star Transgalactic has perfected the art of remote shuttle repairs, thereby removing any need for qualified astronauts. My two girls think I've walked on the moon and at some point I'll have to tell them that I'm just a glorified waiter and concierge. And when I think about how much more this shuttle is capable of, the speed, the independent fuel source, the —

PATRICIA: Let me tell you something, Alex. Life doesn't turn out the way we want it to. You got pretty close to your dream, be thankful for that.

ALEX: That's your advice?

PATRICIA: I wanted to leave some kind of mark on the world, to be remembered for something. I married men who will be remembered. I've outlived them and even though I won't go down in history, I am powerful and I am respected. You take what you get and be glad you're as close to your dream as you are.

ALEX: Goodnight, Patricia.

PATRICIA: Goodnight Alex.

ALEX exits. Lights down briefly. Lights back up on a sleeping PATRICIA. ALEX enters.

ALEX: Morning, Mrs. Lexington. Would you like some tea?

PATRICIA: Mmm…no thank you. Will the sun be out?

ALEX: It should be. I'll deactivate the shade for you.

As soon as he presses the button to deactivate the shade, the room flooded with a bright light that blinks extremely rapidly.

Jesus!

He reactivates the shade.

PATRICIA: What was that?

ALEX: I don't know. I don't — This can't be right, it says our speed is — Just remain calm, Mrs. Lexington, I think the readings are off.

He tries to connect to the station.

This is Peterson, 82QP signing on.

Silence.

Peterson, 82QP do you read me? Mrs. Lexington, I do think you'd be more comfortable in —

PATRICIA: I'm comfortable here.

ALEX: No reason to panic —

PATRICIA: I'm not panicking —

STATION: This is a recording.

ALEX: *(talking over the station recording)* This isn't right —

STATION: I'm afraid I have some difficult news. On February 3, 2030 here on Earth, your shuttle experienced an unexplained and completely unprecedented increase in speed. We have been working for months to determine the cause of this devastating new speed and to devise a way to decelerate the shuttle, but we have been unable to find a safe way to accomplish this. I don't know when you will receive this —

ALEX turns off the message.

PATRICIA: What does he mean, months?

ALEX: This…it's not possible. According to this reading, we're going close to the speed of light, extremely close …

PATRICIA: Is that dangerous?

ALEX: It's — it's — haven't you ever heard of time dilation? No, of course you haven't. Time dilation says the closer you get to traveling at the speed of light, the more time contracts.

PATRICIA: Try me again.

ALEX: Say we're traveling at .9 times the speed of light for one week, more than two weeks would've elapsed back on earth.

PATRICIA: That's a bunch of horseshit.

ALEX: I think I might know better than you.

PATRICIA: So what, while we were asleep a couple of nights went by on earth?

ALEX: (*running calculations on his control board and starting to speak to himself more than to PATRICIA*) According to this we're traveling at .99999999999996 times the speed of light, which would mean one night on the shuttle would equal more than 26 million hours on earth. Roughly…3000 years. But that can't be true. A glitch, maybe…

He starts the message from the station again.

STATION: I don't know when you will receive this message, but, in all likelihood, we will be long gone when you discover the problem. You have the deepest apologies of the former entity known as North Star Transgalactic, the condolences of the President and the world. Your families have been compensated, although

	I know that offers no substitute for what you have lost. A collection of messages from your loved ones will be catalogued and stored on your system. May God be with you.
ALEX:	(*completely stunned*) 3000 years …
PATRICIA:	You're telling me it's the year five thousand thirty?
ALEX:	There are thousands of messages on here.

He selects one.

V/O CHAR.:	Hey, happy Easter!
ALEX:	My wife …
V/O CHAR.:	Today Bryan turned three and, Dad, he looks just like you.

ALEX stops the message.

| ALEX: | It's not my wife, it's my daughter. My girls grew up. They had children. They died. Their children died. Their grandchildren died … |

PATRICIA has walked over and stands in front of the controls.

PATRICIA:	This one just says Loved Ones. Can you play it?

ALEX is in a daze. PATRICIA figures out how to play the message.

| STATION: | Alex and Mrs. Lexington, we brought everyone together, almost 300 of your loved ones here to celebrate your life and legacy. |

The LOVED ONES cheer.

LOVED ONES: *(in unison)* We love you! We miss you! We honor you! We remember you —

ALEX: Turn it off! Turn it off right fucking now!

PATRICIA turns it off.

PATRICIA: What's wrong with you?

ALEX: I can't listen to those — those ghosts!

PATRICIA: They're just people.

ALEX: Not people! Ghosts!

PATRICIA: You're obviously in shock. Just settle down and I think we can sort this out. Get us some water, and we'll talk it over calmly, just me and you.

ALEX: Who the hell else is there!?

PATRICIA: Young man, I need you to —

ALEX: You need me to what? You need me to get you some water? You need me to put a Goddamned freeze-dried chocolate on your pillow? Are you even intelligent enough to grasp the fact that we don't know if human life still exists on Earth? You don't need me to do anything because this job doesn't exist! There's no job! There's no money. I have no children. No family. We're already dead.

He leaves the room.

PATRICIA: Alex?

She pauses, then returns to the controls. She finds a message.

PATRICIA: My son? That's a shocker.

V/O PATRICIA'S SON: Hello Mother. This puts us in an unfortunate position, you being technically alive. We are not able to get control of your estate —

PATRICIA stops the recording and laughs wildly. A ship alarm starts to go off.

V/O SHUTTLE: Exit hatch has been opened during orbit. Seal hatch immediately!

PATRICIA: (*speaking over the V/O SHUTTLE*) Alex! Alex?! Alex!

V/O SHUTTLE Seal hatch immediately! Seal hatch immediately!

PATRICIA struggles to find the right button on the control panel and finally pushes it. The alarm and the V/O SHUTTLE stop.

PATRICIA: (*quietly*) Alex?

She's not sure what to do next. She sits, lost for a moment and realizing she is completely alone. She looks down at the control panel and notices a large group of messages.

Four hundred messages from — My goodness.

V/O YOUNG CHLOE: Hi Grandma. It's me, Chloe! Thank you for the lullaby. I miss the way you smell at Christmas.

> *PATRICIA is touched. She skips through the messages from Chloe until she reaches the last message, spoken by an elderly woman.*

V/O ELDERLY CHLOE:
Hi Grandma. I'm twenty years older than you today. Isn't that something? I've been sick so this recording may be one of my last, but you never know. Perhaps immortality runs in the family. I love you and I hope you're still sleeping peacefully, my grandma in the sky. All my love, Chloe.

> *PATRICIA has been softly weeping during Chloe's message. Then after collecting herself, she looks around for a moment and smiles.*

PATRICIA: (*in awe*) I'm still here.

End of Play

OUT OF INK 2013: Snapshots

Ingredients:

1. The play must contain or involve a photograph — which two or more characters interpret the meaning of differently.
2. One character speaks only in commercial lingo, using known tag-lines or slogans.
3. The play must contain a gunshot or a birth.

The ingredients were contributed by Chris Coleman (then Artistic Director of Center Stage Portland), Ia Ensterä, designer and artist; and Dan Dietz, television writer and former ScriptWorks Artistic Director.

The original production ran June 20-22 and 27-29, 2013 at Salvage Vanguard Theatre, 2803 Manor Rd. in Austin with the following company:

Playwrights: James Burnside, Trey Deason, Amparo Garcia-Crow, Kirk German, Zac Kline, Max Langert, Jason Rainey, and Anne Maria Wynter

Directors: Lowell Bartholomee, Heather Huggins, Ellie McBride, Christina J. Moore, Sharon Sparlin

Performers: Roxy Becker, Pete Betcher, Amy Chang, David DuBose, Nate Dunaway, Joe Hartman, Heather Huggins, Katie Kohler, Jordan Marett, Donald Sneed, Rommel Sulit, and Katy Taylor

Designers: Pam Friday (costumes), George Marsolek (sets and props), Jennifer Rogers (lighting), and Bryan Schneider (sound)

Production Staff:
Stage Manager: Taylor Kulhanek

Asst. Stage Manager: Patti Neff-Tiven
Deck Crew: Joshua Klein
Light Board Operator: Gary Livingston-Weaver
Sound Operator: Dax Taruc

ScriptWorks Staff:
Executive Artistic Director: Christina J. Moore
Member Representative: Max Langert

PLAYDATE
Kirk German
© 2013

CHARACTERS
DEEPAK, 8, *boy, bright and friendly, probably has Asperger's*
SAM, 8, *girl, scrappy, observant, and tough; sort of a tomboy*
SAINT-EXUPERY, 4 ½, *DEEPAK's younger brother, speaks only in slogans and dialogue from cereal commercials*
Note: *Characters do not need to be played by child actors; using adult actors is definitely OK (maybe even better). Also, the ethnic background of the actors is not important.*

SETTING:
The present, a Saturday afternoon. DEEPAK's playroom.

Lights up on two eight-year-olds, DEEPAK and SAM, staring at each other. DEEPAK, smiling, is trying very hard to be welcoming and polite, but he is clearly nervous and out of his element. SAM does not smile back at him. The two children continue to stare at each other for an uncomfortably long period of time without speaking. Finally, DEEPAK clears his throat and breaks the silence.

DEEPAK: Perhaps you did not hear the question?

SAM: No. I heard it.

DEEPAK: Would you like me to repeat it?

SAM: Sure.

DEEPAK: Hello, Sam! Welcome to my playroom. What would you like to do this afternoon?

SAM: I don't care.

DEEPAK: Oh. Ok… I have a lot of games!

SAM: What grade are you in?

DEEPAK: I read at a ninth-grade level.

SAM: That wasn't my question.

DEEPAK: I am eight years old.

SAM: Again, not my question.

DEEPAK: I'm not entirely certain what "grade" I'm in.

SAM: What?

DEEPAK: How old are you?

SAM: Also eight.

DEEPAK: A point of commonality!

SAM: Whatever. Lots of people are eight. Where do you go to school? Liberty Hill? Sunnyside? Blessed Santa Victoria Diez y Bustos de Molina?

DEEPAK: No. Right here!

DEEPAK indicates room. SAM looks around, again unhappy.

SAM: This is your school.

DEEPAK:	Yes. Well, the whole apartment is; that's why they call it "home school."
SAM:	Who calls it that?
DEEPAK:	Everyone. My parents. The other children in the consortium.
SAM:	Other kids come here?
DEEPAK:	No, they have school at their own homes on a daily basis. But we all participate in bi-monthly meet-ups for group enrichment.
SAM:	Where?
DEEPAK:	It varies. Museums, historical societies, planeteria.
SAM:	Field trips.
DEEPAK:	Only one field so far. To observe bees in mating season!
SAM:	So you have friends.
DEEPAK:	Are you referring to the bees?
SAM:	No, the other kids at these "meet-ups."
DEEPAK:	Oh! Yes. I have amicable relationships with several of the other participants. What is your point?
SAM:	My point?! …Why are we doing this? You have your friends. I have my friends. I didn't ask to be set up like this. I don't need a "playdate!" I

	have plenty of friends at school — my <u>normal</u> <u>school</u> that's <u>not</u> in my <u>house</u>!
	Beat.
DEEPAK:	*(unfazed)* Perhaps our mothers felt it would be educational for us?
SAM:	It's Saturday! I don't need to be educated! *(Beat.)* What do you think they're doing right now, anyway?
DEEPAK:	Who?
SAM:	Our moms.
DEEPAK:	Probably talking.
SAM:	Your mom likes talking?
DEEPAK:	Yes. A lot.
SAM:	Yeah. Mine, too.
	Beat.
DEEPAK:	Another point of commonality!
	SAM stares at him. Beat.
DEEPAK:	Would you like to go and listen to what our mothers are talking about?
SAM:	Maybe later.
DEEPAK:	Perhaps I should try a third time?
SAM:	Try what?

DEEPAK clears his throat.

DEEPAK: Hello, Sam! Welcome to my playroom. What would you like to do this aftern —?

SAM: *(interrupting)* You said you have a lot of games?

DEEPAK: Oh, yes!

SAM: Like what?

DEEPAK: Well, the first thing I should tell you is that my family is rather idiosyncratic.

SAM: What's that?

DEEPAK: Unique.

SAM: No kidding.

DEEPAK: Yes. You see, we <u>all</u> <u>very</u> <u>much</u> prefer to play games which provide a legitimate opportunity to shout the <u>name of the game itself</u> out loud!

SAM: OK.

DEEPAK: Preferably when one wins or scores points.

Beat. SAM thinks.

SAM: Like — "Go Fish"?

DEEPAK: *(shouting the name with glee)* GO FISH!!

Beat. SAM is startled. DEEPAK shakes his head.

DEEPAK: No, we don't have that one.

SAM: Oh. Then… like — "Connect Four"?

DEEPAK: *(shouting, while punching his hands into the air)* CONNECT FOUR!! Yes. Good example. We <u>do</u> have that one!

SAM: Uh, Yahtzee?

DEEPAK: YAHTZEE!! Yes. We have that one, too!

> *SAM nods, as if this makes sense, then has an idea.*

SAM: *(half-heartedly)* …Bingo?

DEEPAK: BINGO!! Well, of course! That's the classic, quintessential such game. Bingo! <u>Bingo</u>.

> *SAM raises her fists, speaks a little louder.*

SAM: BINGO! …I <u>WIN</u>!

DEEPAK: Well, in theory. We haven't played yet.

SAM: That's not as weird as I thought it would be… I guess all families have <u>something</u> different about them.

DEEPAK: Oh, yes? Interesting idea… What's different about your family?

SAM: I don't know… Nothing. We have different games at my house. Monopoly, Clue —

DEEPAK: *(interrupting)* <u>CLUE</u>!!!

SAM: *(laughing)* That's awkward. You're supposed to be, like, <u>sneaky</u> in Clue. You can't just shout it.

DEEPAK: MONOPOLY!!

DEEPAK starts laughing, too. Beat.

SAM: SCRABBLE!!

DEEPAK: CHESS!!

As they continue to shout the names of games, SAM goes from mocking the process to unexpectedly enjoying herself.

SAM: LIFE!!

DEEPAK: Hahaha, LIFE!!

SAM: LIFE!!

DEEPAK: LIFE!!

SAM/DEEPAK: *(together)* LIFE!!

During the previous exchange, they have not noticed that ST. EXUPERY has entered; ST. EXUPERY looks around and then suddenly shouts the word at them at a very high volume.

ST. EXUPERY: LIFE!! LIFE!! LIFE!!

SAM freezes, startled by his sudden appearance.

ST. EXUPERY: "LIFE IS FULL OF SURPRISES!!"

SAM: What the —

ST. EXUPERY: *(speaking at a normal volume now and smiling)* "Life Cereal. It's supposed to be good for you."

SAM: Who the hell is _this_ kid??

ST. EXUPERY: "I'm not gonna try it, _you_ try it."

DEEPAK: That's my little brother.

ST. EXUPERY: "Let's get Mikey! He won't eat it. He hates everything."

SAM: Is his name Mikey?

DEEPAK: No. His name is "Saint-Exupery."

ST. EXUPERY: "He likes it! Hey, Mikey!"

DEEPAK: When they adopted him, my parents thought he looked like *The Little Prince*.

SAM: Why does he talk like that?

DEEPAK: I don't know. None of us really know. We're letting him discover his own personality.

ST. EXUPERY: "Make Life cereals part of your balanced, nutritious breakfast!"

DEEPAK: It's a process…

SAM: He watches a lot of TV, huh?

DEEPAK: No. We actually don't own a television. That's just how he's always talked.

ST. EXUPERY: "Follow my nose, it always knows!"

SAM: So… he likes cereal?

ST. EXUPERY: "I'm cuckoo for coco puffs!"

DEEPAK: Hmm. I don't know. He might if he tried it, but our household is 100% gluten-free, so Saint-Exupery and I have never consumed cereal.

SAM: You've <u>never</u> had <u>cereal</u>?

DEEPAK: No, not really. Although, my father <u>does</u> make his own homemade flaxseed paste, which he dehydrates into tiny, hard pellets. We pour raw goat's yogurt over them on cold mornings.

ST. EXUPERY: "They're grrrrrreat!"

DEEPAK: They are <u>not</u> great.

SAM: I hope mom packed me a snack from home…

DEEPAK: Maybe that's what was in the paper bag she gave <u>my</u> mom earlier?

SAM: No, <u>that</u> was Chardonnay.

ST. EXUPERY: "It's magically delicious!"

SAM: I don't get how he knows all this if he's never seen TV or eaten cereal?

ST. EXUPERY: "Silly rabbit —"

DEEPAK: There's a lot about Saint-Exupery that's "mysterious-slash-precocious."

ST. EXUPERY: "Trix are for kids!"

DEEPAK: For example, he creates mixed media art!

ST. EXUPERY: "Gotta have my Pops."

DEEPAK: Saint-Exupery, go get one of your projects to show Sam.

> *ST. EXUPERY looks at them for a long time, then nods and exits. SAM watches him, then looks closely at DEEPAK.*

SAM: How do our moms even know each other?

DEEPAK: I don't know.

SAM: For a smart kid you sure say that a lot.

DEEPAK: You can be smart and still admit that you do not know things.

> *Beat. SAM looks at him, considering what he's just said.*

DEEPAK: What?

SAM: I never thought about that; but I guess it's true.

> *ST. EXUPERY enters holding a toy gun.*

ST. EXUPERY: "Snap! Crackle! Pop —!"

> *ST. EXUPERY pulls the trigger on the gun, which pops out a flag that says "POP!" or "BANG!"*

ST. EXUPERY: "— Rice Krispies!"

He exits again.

DEEPAK: Mom thinks he shows signs of becoming a cutting-edge performance artist.

SAM: What's a performance artist?

DEEPAK: I don't know. On the other hand, our grandma thinks he shows signs of becoming a psycho killer.

SAM: Or maybe a <u>cereal</u> killer! …Get it?…

DEEPAK: …Oh! Wordplay! Very nice. Hmm. I think you're a more advanced eight-year-old than you allow yourself to be.

SAM: Shut up. I'm not. I'm totally normal.

DEEPAK: "Shut up" is rude.

SAM: So I'm rude, get over it. *(Beat.)* Sorry, Deepak. I just — at my school, if you're smarter than the other kids, you — Well, it's just… <u>bad</u>.

DEEPAK: Maybe <u>you</u> should be in home school, too!

SAM: I'd rather die.

DEEPAK: No, you wouldn't, you're exaggerating. Hey, maybe that's what our moms are talking about!

SAM: I don't think so. My mom's not exactly qualified to be my teacher. Plus she has a full-time job.

DEEPAK: What about your dad?

SAM: It's just me and mom.

DEEPAK: Oh.

ST. EXUPERY enters with a large collage.

ST. EXUPERY: "Honeycomb's big, yeah, yeah, yeah; it's not small, no, no, no!"

SAM: This is not like <u>any</u> other playdate I've been to.

DEEPAK: Me neither. See, we <u>are</u> being educated!

SAM: (*rolling her eyes, but smiling nonetheless*) Great…

ST. EXUPERY: "I'm the master rapper and I'm here to say, I love Fruity Pebbles in a major way!"

DEEPAK: He wants you to look at his picture.

SAM: OK.

ST. EXUPERY hands SAM the collage. SAM and DEEPAK lean in and look at it together.

SAM: Oh. This is — really neat. Look at that. Wow — I. I like it. I really — <u>love</u> it, Mikey.

DEEPAK: His name is Saint-Exup —

SAM: Mikey's easier to say.

DEEPAK: Can you tell what the photos are?

SAM: I think so… It's so pretty the way he put it all together.

She starts to identify various pieces and point at them.

SAM: The eye of a housefly. Something furry, maybe the skin of a coconut? A fish scale. And a raindrop? A... oh, a rose thorn. The vein of a leaf. A butterfly wing. A whisker...

Beat. SAM stares at it for a moment, strangely emotional.

DEEPAK: Is it making you sad?

SAM: No. ...Look — the edge of a sand dollar!

DEEPAK: You're good at this.

SAM: And a raisin? Or maybe a coffee bean? No, a raisin.

DEEPAK: I think that's a dried jalapeño.

SAM: Pretty sure it's a raisin.

DEEPAK: I don't know... We have a lot of peppers hanging in our kitchen, and —

SAM: Mikey! What is this?

ST. EXUPERY: "Two scoops of plump, juicy raisins... in Kellogg's Raisin Bran!"

DEEPAK: That's as close to an answer as we'll get.

SAM: So I win...!

DEEPAK: It's not a competition.

SAM: It is if I shout the game's name.

DEEPAK: What game?

> *Beat. SAM looks at him.*

SAM: PLAYDATE!

> *Beat. DEEPAK smiles.*

DEEPAK: PLAYDATE!

SAM: PLAYDATE!!

DEEPAK: PLAYDATE!!

SAM: PLAYDATE!!!

> *SAM and DEEPAK continue shouting "PLAYDATE!" one on top of the other, more and more exuberantly and exaggeratedly. ST. EXUPERY, curious, watches them. He smiles. Lights out.*

End of Play

OUT OF INK 2014: The Empty Set

Ingredients:

1. A pair of mismatched failures.
2. Peering into the void.
3. Mathematical errors.

The ingredients were contributed by Brad Carlin, Managing Director of the Fusebox Festival, Jennifer Haley, playwright and ScriptWorks Core Alum, and Ellie McBride, director and performer.

The original production ran June 12-14 and 19-21, 2014 at the Trinity Street Theatre, 901 Trinity St., 4th Floor, in Austin with the following company:

Playwrights: Lowell Bartholomee, Allison Orr Block, Carolyn Kennedy, Max Langert, Jason Rainey, Nettie Reynolds, Sheila Lynch Rinear, and Cindy Vining

Dramaturg: Teresa Stankiewicz

Directors: Carolyn Kennedy, Max Langert, Ellie McBride Christina J. Moore, Linda Nenno, and Sharon Sparlin

Performers: Suzanne Balling, Roxy Becker, Amy Chang, David DuBose, Rachel Hoovler, Joshua Klein, Max Langert, Ellie McBride, Christi Moore, Garry Peters, and Gricelda Silva

Designers: Pam Friday (costumes), Natalie George (lights), Julia Phipps (sets/props), and Josean Rodriguez with Eliot Kingsley Haynes (sound)

Production Staff:
Stage Manager: Taylor Kulhanek

Asst. Stage Manager:	Julia Phipps
Technical Director	Zac Crofford
Light Board Operator:	Taylor Kulhanek
Sound Operator:	Josean Rodriguez
Deck Crew:	Joshua Klein

ScriptWorks Staff:
Executive Artistic Director:	Christina J. Moore
Member Representative:	Max Langert

IT'S TIME
Max Langert
©2014

CHARACTERS:
LISA, *16, smart, rebellious, passionate*
KAREN, *16, cautious, loyal, likes music*
MS. HARPER, *40-something math teacher*
MS. LIVINGSTON, *40-something art teacher*

SETTING:
A high school classroom on a Friday night.

We hear the song "Stairway to Heaven" in the background coming from the gymnasium some distance off.

LISA is here pacing anxiously. She's decked out in funky threads circa 1982. Untucked shirt, asymmetrical hair, splashes of neon here and there. She's a hip chick (for 1982).

There's a blackboard on wheels behind her. And behind that is some kind of wooden contraption we can't quite see. As the music changes to something else (Howard Jones?), the door opens and KAREN enters in a hurry.

KAREN is more buttoned up than LISA. Hair is symmetrical, she seems straight-laced, clothes probably from the Gap. LISA turns to her.

LISA: What took you so long?

KAREN: I had to finish dancing.

LISA: With Kevin?

KAREN: Yeah.

LISA: Why?

KAREN: Because he asked me. Because we came to the dance together.

LISA: *(annoyed)* So stupid.

KAREN: Plus that song is like eighteen minutes long.

Beat.

KAREN: Anyway…

LISA: Did anyone see you come in?

KAREN: No.

LISA: You're sure?

KAREN: Yes.

LISA goes to KAREN and looks at her. Their expressions soften slowly and they soon embrace romantically, stroking each other's hair with affection, their guards coming down.

Then KAREN's ears perk up.

KAREN: Hey, I like this beat!

She pulls away from LISA and starts dancing, trying to get LISA to dance with her. LISA just looks at her skeptically and shakes her head. KAREN slows down and eventually stops.

KAREN: (*self-consciously*) Anyway…

LISA: Hey, I've got something to show you.

KAREN: (*intrigued*) Ooh.

LISA: It's over here.

> *LISA goes over to the wooden contraption and pulls it out. It's wobbly and messy and big enough for two people to stand in, at least up to their waists.*

KAREN: (*perplexed*) What is it?

LISA: Our future.

KAREN: What?

LISA: This is how we're gonna be happy, Karen.

KAREN: (*touches LISA*) But I *am* happy, Lisa.

LISA: Together, Karen. Happy *together*.

> *KAREN's brow furrows as she examines the box-like thing more carefully.*

LISA: I'm so sick of the rules in this town and all the dirty looks everyone gives you if you're just a little bit different, you know? There's nothing here for us.

KAREN: I know. And that's why we're going to leave after we graduate. Just like we talked about.

LISA: Graduate from high school?

KAREN: Yeah.

LISA: And what about art school after that? I know you want to go.

KAREN: Well, we'll see about that. We said we'd talk about it later. There's plenty of time left.

LISA: No there isn't. Time is running out. Look at me, Karen. I love you.

KAREN: (*tentatively, after glancing around to see if anyone's looking*) I love you too.

LISA: I want you to come with me.

KAREN: Come with you where? I can't leave Texas. You know that. Everything I know is here.

LISA: I'm not saying leave Texas. I'm saying leave Now.

KAREN: (*shakes head, confused*) I don't understand.

LISA: Leave the *present*. In the future things will be better. That's what I'm saying. Things are improving slowly. It's just taking too long for us to sit around and wait. We have to do something. We'll be too old before real progress comes. That's why we gotta grab the bull by the balls now while we have the chance.

KAREN: I still don't get it.

LISA: Karen.

KAREN: What.

LISA: *(about the box)* I built this.

KAREN: Okay.

LISA: It's a machine, all right? A time machine.

KAREN laughs. But LISA is dead serious.

KAREN: You're crazy.

LISA: No, I'm not. I mean yes, I am. But this is real. What I built. I worked it out.

KAREN: Worked it out how?

LISA: In woodshop. And in calculus. All those AP courses, they really paid off. And advanced physics, man, that was a serious eye-opener.

KAREN: *(digesting this)* Okay. So you're saying you built a time machine. In woodshop. And in calculus and whatever. And what do you want to do with it?

LISA: I want to leave. With you. Now. And go thirty years into the future. Things are starting to change, don't you see? Ann Richards just won the election for state treasurer. Some people are saying she might even be governor one day.

KAREN eyes her skeptically.

LISA: Think about it. In 30 years we won't be able to recognize this town. No one will blink an eye about two girls — two women — being in love. I bet we'll even be able to get married.

KAREN: Oh please.

LISA: By 2012 we might even have the first black... secretary of state.

KAREN: You're dreaming.

LISA: Come on, baby. Let's do it. What have we got to lose?

> *KAREN mulls this for a moment as LISA reaches for her hand. KAREN looks at LISA's hand and cautiously embraces it. LISA beams as they both step into the wooden contraption and LISA begins fiddling with knobs on the dashboard. As she does the lights around us begin to flicker and we hear the sounds of an engine starting to churn. KAREN is wide-eyed, nervous, excited.*
>
> *Then suddenly the door to the classroom flies open and their math teacher, MS. HARPER, enters.*

MS. HARPER: *(breathless)* There you are!

> *LISA and KAREN are surprised to see her. But LISA continues to fiddle with knobs, determined.*

LISA: You can't stop us, Ms. Harper. It's too late.

MS. HARPER: Don't do it. Please. You'll regret it.

> *Lights continue to flicker as the engine noise gets louder and louder. The machine begins to shake.*

LISA: Karen, hang on!

KAREN: Oh God! (*clings to LISA*)

MS. HARPER: Wait! Listen to me! I don't want to stop you. I want to *help* you!

LISA: You can help us by stepping back. I don't know what kind of kick this thing is going to have and I don't want you to get hurt.

MS. HARPER: You don't understand. Your formula. There's a mistake!

LISA: (*shakes her head*) Impossible.

MS. HARPER: Listen to me!

> *She runs to the blackboard and flips it over. On the other side we see an elaborate mathematic equation. LISA and KAREN pay attention. LISA slows down with the fiddling. The lights go back to normal and the engine begins to quiet.*
>
> *MS. HARPER points to a spot on the board where there's a series of numbers clustered.*

MS. HARPER: Here.

LISA: It's all correct, Ms. Harper.

MS. HARPER: No. It's not. You have the negative and positive sign swapped here, see? Instead of going *ahead* thirty years, you're about to go *back* thirty years. To 1952.

> *KAREN eyes LISA nervously.*

> *LISA stops the machine completely and steps out, goes to the board.*

LISA: (*examining the evidence*) Well, look at that.

> *KAREN storms over.*

KAREN: I thought you knew what you were doing!

LISA: I did. I do.

KAREN: 1952?! Do you have any idea how awful that would be? Michael Jackson wasn't even born yet!

LISA: (*to MS. HARPER, about the equation*) How did you know?

MS. HARPER: I saw some of your notes in class and figured it out.

KAREN: (*to LISA*) I can't believe you!

LISA: I'm sorry, okay? I'm sorry.

MS. HARPER: Things were a lot tougher for people like you in the 50's.

KAREN: I can't even imagine.

LISA: (*defensively*) What do you mean, "people like you"?

MS. HARPER: Just you two. You know. What you have. Your situation.

LISA: (*relaxing a bit*) Yeah.

MS. HARPER: You couldn't hold hands back then, be alone together anywhere. You've at least got some privacy and rights now. Are you sure you want to give all that up to go into an uncertain future?

LISA and KAREN look at each other, smile.

LISA: We're sure.

KAREN nods.

MS. HARPER: Okay. If you just flip the sign around here and make a few changes to your controls, it should work. *(edits the equation on the blackboard)*

LISA goes to the contraption and starts fiddling some more. MS. HARPER goes over to help her. They fiddle together.

LISA: *(about controls)* Like this?

MS. HARPER: Yeah, that should do it.

KAREN: You fixed it?

MS. HARPER: Looks good.

LISA: *(to KAREN)* Are you ready?

KAREN: *(to MS. HARPER)* You're sure?

MS. HARPER nods.

LISA and KAREN step back in the contraption and LISA fiddles some more. Lights blink, engine revs. Louder and louder until takeoff. The box shakes and shimmies,

> *and the girls brace and hang on the best they can. Soon they're soaring off into the future.*
>
> *Lights change as they're in a kind of black space. They're all alone, zipping and zooming through space.*

KAREN: I'm scared.

LISA: I know, baby. It's going to be all right, though. I promise.

KAREN: I'm so glad Ms. Harper was there.

LISA: Yeah, that was a close one.

KAREN: She was so nice. Seemed so concerned about us. It's almost like…

LISA: What?

KAREN: Nothing. I know she's got a husband and a kid and all that.

> *More zooming and zipping. LISA checks the controls. The contraption starts slowing and eventually stops. They're still in a kind of blackness.*

LISA: I think we made it.

KAREN: To the future? Already?

LISA: Yeah. Let me just put this thing in standby mode. Then I'll go check.

KAREN: Standby mode? You thought of everything.

LISA: AP classes. Don't knock 'em.

LISA steps off, walks a few feet to the edge of the stage and peers off deeply. As things come into focus her expression changes. From concern to disbelief to horror. She runs back to the machine.

KAREN: What is it? Is it 1952?

LISA: No. 2012. The date is right.

KAREN: But?

LISA: I was peering into the Texas legislative building. It's even worse than 1982. I can't believe it. You should see some of the bills they're considering.

LISA starts fiddling with knobs again.

KAREN: What are you doing?

LISA: Recalibrating. Thirty more years.

KAREN: 2042?

LISA: Bingo.

KAREN: Oh God.

And blastoff. Lights, engine, they fly off.

Now the lights shift back to the classroom where MS. HARPER has been. Back in 1982 where we left off. MS. HARPER looks worried, glancing off into the distance, imagining what must be happening. In a moment the door opens and MS. LIVINGSTON enters.

MS. LIVINGSTON: There you are.

MS. HARPER: Yeah.

MS. LIVINGSTON: You found them?

MS. HARPER: I did.

MS. LIVINGSTON: How did it go?

MS. HARPER: They're off.

MS. LIVINGSTON: Into the future?

MS. HARPER nods.

MS. LIVINGSTON: *(considers this)* How do you think it'll go?

MS. HARPER looks at MS. LIVINGSTON for a moment. Then reaches out and touches her hand.

MS. HARPER: I want to have hope.

MS. LIVINGSTON looks at MS. HARPER's hand and cautiously embraces it. Smiles at MS. HARPER affectionately.

Suddenly a P.A. system crackles to life in the speakers overhead.

VOICE: All staff, please report to the gymnasium at once. We're about to crown the king and queen of the dance.

MS. LIVINGSTON pulls away from MS. HARPER and moves toward the exit.

MS. LIVINGSTON: We should probably go. They'll wonder about us.

MS. HARPER nods. MS. LIVINGSTON exits. MS. HARPER takes a deep breath, looks off into space again, and exits too.

Lights shift to LISA and KAREN and the time machine. They've landed again.

LISA: Made it. 2042.

LISA walks off and peers again into the distance. Her expression goes from concern to a kind of cautious optimism. She returns to the machine.

KAREN: Well?

LISA: I think this is better. Things are looking up.

KAREN: Oh good. Finally.

LISA: It's hot out there, though. Wish we'd thought to bring Coppertone.

She reaches for KAREN's hand. KAREN looks down at it, then embraces it just as MS. LIVINGSTON had with MS. HARPER.

KAREN: It's time. Let's go.

They look at each other for a moment, smile at each other, then run off into the future, full of hope.

Lights slowly down.

End of Play

OUT OF INK 2015: Random Acts of Magic

Ingredients:

1. A piece of magic.
2. Two characters must switch clothes/costumes at least once during the play.
3. A character must revisit the most embarrassing day of their life.

The ingredients were contributed by University of Texas faculty and ScriptWorks Advisory Board member, Liz Engelman, One Minute Play Festival Artistic Director, Dominic D'Andrea, and costume designer, Pam Friday.

The original production was at Hyde Park Theatre, 511 W. 43rd St. in Austin, April 23-25 and April 30-May 2, 2015 with the following company:

Playwrights: Rita Anderson, Kirk German, Carolyn Kennedy, Max Langert, Briandaniel Oglesby, Sarah Saltwick, Samuel Vaughan, and Cindy Vining

Directors: Lowell Bartholomee, Carolyn Kennedy, Linda Nenno, Sharon Sparlin, and Lily Wolff

Performers: David DuBose, Marie Fahlgren, Joe Hartman, Gina Houston, Carolyn Kennedy, Matrex Kilgore, Jenny Lavery, Noah Martin, Lori Navarrete, Zac Thomas, Robin Grace Thompson, and Minerva Villa

Designers: Natalie George (sets, props, & lighting), Jessica Gilzow (costumes), Jason Newman (sound)

Production Staff:
Stage Manager: Patti Neff-Tiven
Assistant Stage Manager: Elizabeth Miller

Light Board Operator: Zachary Yoke
Sound Operator: Patti Neff-Tiven
Electricians: Dallas Tate, Zachary Yoke

ScriptWorks Staff:
Executive Artistic Director: Christina J. Moore
Member Representative: Max Langert

THE DISAPPEARING ROSE TRICK

Briandaniel Oglesby
© 2015

CHARACTERS

ROSA
JOANA
GRACIELA
WOLF

ROSA: Once upon a time there were three sisters

JOANA: One

GRACIELA: Two

ROSA: Three

JOANA: Joanna.

GRACIELA: The older one

ROSA: The ancient one.

GRACIELA: Graciela.

JOANA: The middle child.

ROSA: The wicked middle child.

JOANA and GRACIELA:
And then there's —

ROSA: Rosa.

JOANA and GRACIELA:
The baby

ROSA: *I am not a baby.*

JOANA: Graciela, she is, well —

GRACIELA: I am the pretty one.

JOANA:	ROSA:
Define "pretty?"	That's what she thinks.

GRACIELA: Shut up. Both of you.

JOANA: And Joana is the smart one

ROSA:	GRACIELA:
She says that because she wears glasses	She's says that because she's valedictorian

JOANA: Valedictorian. Woodland High. Class of '72.

ROSA: Told you she's old.

JOANA: Two years — whatever —

GRACIELA: And Rosa —

ROSA: And me, I'm —

JOANA and GRACIELA:
 The one who lies

ROSA: *You are so mean to me.*

JOANA and GRACIELA:
 One, two, three.

ROSA: I hate you.

JOANA: And these three sisters.

GRACIELA: Their childhood —

JOANA: — are reared, grow up, come of age in

ALL: Woodland.

JOANA:	GRACIELA	ROSA
A small town	A shitty ugly city squat	an enchanted land
A suburb of Sacramento	in the fields of Northern	*an enchanted land*
It has an ag and factory-based economy	California	
	Seriously, Rosa?	What?

JOANA: The home — tiny

GRACIELA: A hovel.

ROSA: A peasant's cottage —

JOANA: Two rooms. It's painted nice — bright yellow —

GRACIELA: but it's a nothing / shack

JOANA	ROSA
A humble house	It's *literally* a peasant's cottage.

GRACIELA: On the worst street, in the worst part of town

ALL: Olive Drive

JOANA: Even if you have the nicest house in the worst part of town, you got problems.

GRACIELA: A dragon, right Rosa? A big black, scaly dragon, breathing fire and unhappiness, that's what we got to deal with, right Rosa?

ROSA: You are so mean to me. You are literally the most wicked in all the land.

JOANA: Olive Drive is wrapped up by crappy alleys, a couple / abandoned houses

GRACIELA: Like crack dens —

JOANA: a blown out gas station-turned tienda, Crest View Apartments, the old clapboard house where Pedro works on shell of a Mustang. The street sits next to the train tracks.

GRACIELA and ROSA:
Chk-chk-chk-chk-chk

JOANA: Every morning, they smell the diesel.

GRACIELA and ROSA smell it.

GRACIELA: And in this tiny enchanted house cottage hovel whatever.

JOANA: Mama collects knickknacks. Trinkets. Five and dime. Garage sales. Thrift shops. Teacups. Magnets shaped like food. Porcelain roosters.

GRACIELA: A shit-ton of this crap.

ROSA: A dragon's horde.

JOANA: The wealth of poverty.

ROSA: So many tiny, magical items. And the most magical of all — Abuelo's old crucifix hanging in the kitchen.

GRACIELA: Watching over us. Keeping us out of trouble.

JOANA: Watching us get into trouble.

ROSA: I am literally their slave in our peasant cottage.

JOANA: She isn't

GRACIELA: She really isn't

JOANA: The sisters don't get along. Sibling rivalries are the byproduct of having multiple children. Distribution of resources —

GRACIELA: All that shit.

JOANA: If there's enough, the kids are spoiled; if there isn't enough, the kids scrap for everything.

GRACIELA: There isn't enough.

ROSA: I am their slave. They are literally wicked stepsisters.

JOANA and GRACIELA:
We aren't stepsisters.

ROSA: They pick on me all the time.

> *Boom, we're in scene. And GRACIELA is pissed.*

GRACIELA: Rosa!

ROSA: What?

GRACIELA: You're wearing my camisola!

ROSA: No, it's mine.

GRACIELA: Rosa, Rosa, menti-rosa!

ROSA: Aya! I am not lying.

GRACIELA: Give it back.

ROSA: IT'S MINE

And she runs away

GRACIELA: Don't you run away from me.

GRACIELA follows.

JOANA: And she runs away. Graciela catches her, outside in the alley, there she is, hiding behind an old refrigerator.

GRACIELA: YOU FAT THIEF! THINK YOU CAN GET AWAY FROM ME! YOU'RE GOING TO STRETCH IT, GORDITA!

JOANA: And then the neighbors — Pedro and his amigos Pepe and El Moreno, these three gorgeous boys, you can see their chonies up up up their slender hipbones, they are working on the shell of the Mustang, and Señora Moscatela opens her door. All are watching.
And I say: what's going on?

GRACIELA: Rosa, that was a gift. Nardo gave me that camisola, you're going to infect it with your smell and your ugly

JOANA: And Rosa looks at her sister, as if for help.

ROSA: I don't have nothing nice.

JOANA: What she should know is that Joana is the worst, but seems the best.

ROSA: Joana.

JOANA: She should know that Joana is the wicked one.

ROSA: JOANA!

JOANA: Under the eyes of El Señor, Rosa. Mira, ya ve.

GRACIELA: Abuelo's carved crucifix hanging in the kitchen — watching us through the kitchen window.

JOANA: You keep stealing under the eyes of Jesus, Rosa. Maldita en los ojos del Padre. Give it to her now.

ROSA: The neighbors are watching.

GRACIELA: BECAUSE YOU STOLE MY BEST THING!

JOANA: Rosa. Return it.

ROSA: But, the neighbors!

JOANA: This is your penance.

ROSA: This is the most embarrassing moment of my life!

JOANA: And in that moment, as the neighbors, as Pedro with his chonies are watching, she lifts her shirt

> *She takes off the camisole. There are bruises on her back. She hands it to her sister.*

ROSA: Take it.

JOANA: And there

GRACIELA: And then.

JOANA: In the alley on Olive Drive.

GRACIELA: Under the eyes of El Niño hanging from the cross and beautiful neighbor boys and Señora Moscatela

JOANA: something happens that can never be taken back.

ROSA: So, later that night.

GRACIELA: chk chk chk chk chk chk chk

JOANA: The train brings someone to town.

ROSA is grumpily taking out the trash.

ROSA: Rosa! Take out the trash, Rosa. Aya! Rosa is not your *slave*, Graciela.

A howl.

ROSA: Who's afraid of the Big Bad Wolf, the Big Bad Wolf, the Big Bad Wolf.
Who's afraid of the Big Bad Wolf.

WOLF: Tra-la-la-la-la.

The WOLF appears. He's dapper. Well, dapperish. He's smoking. In more than one sense. The smoke from his cigarette swirls around him like fog.

WOLF: Hello, little girl.

ROSA: Hello.

The WOLF scratches.

ROSA: You're a wolf.

> *The WOLF stops. How did she know?*

WOLF: I am. No one sees that. You must be special.

ROSA: I'm not special.

WOLF: What special wolf-seeing powers you have, little girl. Hmmm. Make a wish.

> *The WOLF magically produces a bundle of roses from his sleeves.*

ROSA: Roses.

WOLF: Roses for Rosa.

ROSA: You know my name.

WOLF: And you know I'm a wolf.

ROSA: Let me pet you.

WOLF: Wolves like to be petted.

> *ROSA pets the WOLF.*

ROSA: Pet me back.

> *The WOLF pets her back.*
> *Damn. Like damn.*

WOLF: You know. I'm wolf — and I'm magic.

> *He pulls out something else…. but what?*
> *Something only she can see.*

ROSA: Oh.

WOLF: I'll make you a princess. I'm wolf royalty, you know. If you come with me.

ROSA: You think you're stealing me. I'm stealing you.

Do they kiss?

WOLF: I want to swallow you, my princess. I want to eat you whole, make you a part of me.

ROSA: I'll be inside you. I'll be safe. And you'll carry me away....

WOLF: Tralalala.

GRACIELA: Rosa! Get in here! Bedtime!

WOLF is gone.

ROSA: She tells the sisters about the magical wolf.

JOANA: You're literally, literally the girl who cried wolf.

GRACIELA:	JOANA:
Are you high?	Are you drunk?
I can smell it on her.	I can smell it on her.
Are you insane?	Are you stupid?
She's acting crazy.	She's not the smart one.
Are you fucking kidding us?	

ROSA: He is.

JOANA: A magic wolf prince? What the hell. Grow the fuck up.

ROSA: You are so mean.

GRACIELA: The sisters — say they don't believe her.

> *The WOLF howls in the distance. GRACIELA and ROSA look. We see his silhouette. He disappears.*

GRACIELA: Let's get back to sleep.

JOANA: And… we sleep.

> *A beat.*

GRACIELA: Then, something wakes us.

JOANA: The train passing at a time when it's not supposed to pass.

GRACIELA: Chk chk chk chk chk chk

> *A scream. It's ROSA!*

JOANA: Where's Rosa?

GRACIELA: Where did the crucifix go?

JOANA: The train passes.

GRACIELA: There she is!

JOANA: Chk chk chk chk chk chk.

> *We see ROSA and the WOLF.*
> *The train passes.*
> *ROSA disappears.*
> *The WOLF smacks his lips.*
> *He's eaten ROSA.*
> *He flosses with the crucifix.*
> *Then — he's gone.*

Beat.

Beat.

GRACIELA: The most embarrassing moment of her life.

JOANA: The most embarrassing moment in my life is ten years later. I am in grad school, and I'm on a bus,

We're suddenly on a bus.

JOANA: and *everyone* on this bus is avoiding looking at each other. This isn't one of those, grudgingly friendly buses.
And I see him.

The WOLF is on the bus.

JOANA: Or I think I see him — and all I can think is, it's the wolf. The wolf who took my sister. And then I'm shouting, STOP THE BUS! WOLF WOLF WOLF! THE WOLF THAT ATE MY SISTER IS ON THE BUS!

The bus lurches to a stop. Everyone falls.

And they're all on this sticky grimy floor, and an old woman starts crying, and I'm pointing pointing pointing — and everyone is looking at me, including the gentleman who suddenly looks very human, and the human he resembles is not the wolf I saw that night.
And everyone is looking at me, and I want to tell them —
But no words come.

I want to call my sister, maybe she'll make it better, but Graciela doesn't feel embarrassment these days, not with her pills.

I'm pretty sure the man on the bus is a wolf, though. Just not *the* wolf.

GRACIELA: There are too many wolves out there.

JOANA: Once upon a time there were three sisters

GRACIELA: One

JOANA: Who is oh, so pretty.

GRACIELA: Two

JOANA: Oh, so smart.

GRACIELA: And.

JOANA: A third.

GRACIELA: Who is —

JOANA: One
Two

Blackout.

WOLF: Tra-la-la-la-la

End of Play

OUT OF INK 2016: Carry On

Ingredients:

1. All props and scenery must be able to fit into, and include, a carry-on suitcase.
2. A character in the play must write a note for another character which the audience never gets to hear.
3. The sound of the land.

The ingredients were contributed by Obie award-winning playwright Caridad Svich, scene designer and Co-Director of Paper Chairs, Lisa Laratta, and Rude Mechs Co-Producing Artistic Director and Head of Playwriting and Directing at the University of Texas, Kirk Lynn.

The original production ran April 28-30 and May 5-7, 2016 at Hyde Park Theatre, 511 W. 43rd St. in Austin with the following company:

Playwrights: Katherine Catmull, Carolyn Kennedy, Briandaniel Oglesby, Sheila Lynch Rinear, Adam Sweeney, Lisa B. Thompson, Megan Thornton, and Anne Maria Wynter

Directors: Caleb Britton, Ellie McBride, Christina J. Moore, Linda Nenno, and Rudy Ramirez

Performers: Roxy Becker, Zac Carr, Kristin Chiles, David DuBose, Jennifer John, Michael Joplin, Matrex Kilgore, Taji Senior, Johanna Whitmore

Designers: Lowell Bartholomee (sound), Pam Friday (costumes), Shelby Gebhart (lighting), and Brooks Naylor (props)

Production Staff:
Stage Manager: Brianna Veselka

Asst. Stage Manager:	Joshua Klein
Light Board Operator:	Matt Murphy
Sound Operator:	Brianna Veselka
Electrician:	Matt Murphy

ScriptWorks Staff:

Executive Artistic Director:	Christina J. Moore
Member Representative:	Max Langert

WATCH
Lisa B. Thompson
© 2016

CHARACTERS

BLACK WOMAN, *thirty-five years old, brown skin, average build. She possesses a spirit of optimism. Wearing jean overalls, a black cotton tee-shirt and hoop earrings. Barefoot. She is disarmingly beautiful. Known as Subject 1640, code name Virginia.*
SCIENTIST 1, *wearing a white lab coat, mask and gloves. Has a bitter personality.*
SCIENTIST 2, *wearing a white lab coat, mask and gloves. Has a very even keel persona.*
SCIENTIST 3, *wearing a white lab coat, mask and gloves. Has an enthusiastic personality.*

Morning in the distant or near future. A white room in a corporate/government run scientific lab in North America. At this point in history the government and corporations are clearly "united" under one purpose —control of the entire population for the cultural, social and financial benefit of a select few. The lab has a glass enclosure with BLACK WOMAN inside. The SCIENTISTS stand outside the room observing BLACK WOMAN as she writes a daily note to her observers. The SCIENTISTS are each wearing masks and gloves that conceal their race, age and gender.

SCIENTIST 1: My mind is going numb. This is so dull. She isn't doing *anything* of importance. How long has it been writing so far?

SCIENTIST 2: (*taking notes on a hand-held electronic device*) Only 23 minutes, 49 seconds.

SCIENTIST 1: Kill me now.

SCIENTIST 2: Oh stop. I told you months ago that you should apply to work in Sector 17. You just don't appreciate the art of observation.

SCIENTIST 1: The art of observation Please! You know what —

SCIENTIST 3 enters with gushing enthusiasm.

SCIENTIST 3: Good morning!

SCIENTIST 1: *(monotone)* Morning.

SCIENTIST 2: Welcome. I didn't know you were with us today.

SCIENTIST 3: Yes, I'm supposed to visit each lab over the new few weeks so I can get a sense of the operation. *(checks a small electronic device)* Yep, June 19. Today is my visit to Lab 1.863.

SCIENTIST 1: What do you think?

SCIENTIST 3: Fantastic! I love it. The work is fascinating. My last assignment was in Sector B1888 — Rio, so this is quite a change.

SCIENTIST 2: Not many of them left down there either, right?

SCIENTIST 3: No, but there are a lot more of them in South America. I guess they like the weather better. *(beat)* Sorry, I didn't get a chance to review the report. What is the duration of this morning's observation?

SCIENTIST 1: Too long. I'm so bored.

SCIENTIST 3: Really? I find this truly fascinating. *(stands closer to the window)*

SCIENTIST 1: Are you serious? Fascinating? Right.

SCIENTIST 3: Yes it is. She's one of the last ones. I'm sorry — the duration?

SCIENTIST 2: The protocol is 60 minutes at 8am, 2pm, and at 8pm. There is also a random 10-minute observation in the middle of the night sometime between midnight and 5am.

SCIENTIST 3: *(typing notes on electronic device)* Ok. Got it. And this experiment is supposed to allow us to…?

SCIENTIST 2: We don't know why. The orders are pretty basic: just watch, observe, take notes and create the report.

SCIENTIST 1: Mind numbing! Can you believe they're spending all this funding on her? For an entire year!

SCIENTIST 2: *(to SCIENTIST 1)* Will you please be professional for once in your life? *(to SCIENTIST 3)* The protocol manual states we are to observe the subject for twelve months to determine her "physical fitness, mental abilities and emotional well-being."

SCIENTIST 3: What month is this?

SCIENTIST 1: Three, seven, nine? Does it matter? It's pretty much the same damn thing every day.

SCIENTIST 2: Language! Pull yourself together. *(to SCIENTIST 3)* We are now in the fourth month of observation.

SCIENTIST 3: She beings each day writing a note to "her captor," whatever that means.

SCIENTIST 2: This species is nearly extinct.

SCIENTST 1: That's no surprise. Look at her. Watch for ten minutes and tell me if you're still "fascinated." It's not only boring but a bit…

SCIENTIST 2: She is a bit cagey.

SCIENTIST 3: Well, she's kinda in a cage, so…

SCIENTIST 2: It's actually an enclosure. The protocol manual describes it as a —

SCIENTIST 1: Ok. We get it. It's a nice cage.

SCIENTIST 3: Right. Of course.

SCIENTIST 2: Twenty-five more minutes.

SCIENTIST 1: Oh God!

SCIENTIST 3: And then? Once the observation window closes what do we do?

SCIENTIST 2: We submit our report and then set up everything for the afternoon observation.

SCIENTIST 3: Sounds easy enough.

Earthquake shakes the room. The SCIENTISTS barely take note of it.

BLACK WOMAN looks up from writing until the rumbling subsides.

SCIENTIST 1: Easy. Yep. I'm sure she *(pointing to BLACK WOMAN)* could even manage it.

BLACK WOMAN begins to softly sing a spiritual. Her song is nearly inaudible, yet recognizable.

SCIENTIST 3: What can I do to help? I'm sure I could —

SCIENTIST 2: Watch!

SCIENTIST 3: Yes. I know, I just —

BLACK WOMAN has stopped writing. She folds the note, places it on the floor by the partition separating her from the SCIENTISTS.

SCIENTIST 2: No, watch! *(Wildly pointing at BLACK WOMAN whose humming has become louder. After she finishes, she beings to pray.)*

SCIENTIST 3: Whoa! *(typing notes)*

SCIENTIST 1: Nothing new. Just like clockwork.

SCIENTIST 3: Well I'm pretty impressed. I never saw one in action.

SCIENTIST 1: That's nothing remarkable.

SCIENTIST 3: Why is she doing that? She's completely alone.

SCIENTIST 2: *(looking through a booklet)* Spiritual sustenance. It says during slavery, their songs were a major coping mechanism.

SCIENTIST 3: It's absolutely beautiful. *(They all stop to listen.)* I read this in my history class.

SCIENTIST 1: Fantastic! Now everyone's an expert on a soon to be extinct people.

SCIENTIST 2: It's a long cultural tradition. It developed into an entire musical genre. *(reading from the electronic device's screen)* Those sorrow songs became the field holler which morphed into the blues and then the blues became jazz and then jazz became funk and then…Hmm. What's "t-werking?"

SCIENTIST 3: I think I heard that kind of music at my grandmother's house once. It's very loud and…rhythmic.

SCIENTIST 1: Why do you two care about this? Just do your job and enjoy your time away from this place.

SCIENTIST 3: What do you mean?

SCIENTIST 1: They used to be *(whispers)* slaves. Got it? If you ask me, they were segregated from the normal population for a reason. So we're supposed to care because they are nearly extinct now?

SCIENTIST 2: Why do you even work here?

SCIENTIST 1: Good question. To be honest I have student loans to pay off. The senior scientist salary is good and when I leave here each day my work is done.

SCIENTIST 2: How honorable.

SCIENTIST 1: I'm just saying if the male of their species doesn't care, then why should we? It's just a job. How much longer?

SCIENTIST 2: Read the clock yourself! I'm not your assistant.

SCIENTST 3: You two fighting is making her laugh. You're amusing her somehow.

SCIENTIST 1: She doesn't know she's being observed. From what I understand this room is soundproof. She's just laughing for her own reasons. Crazy I guess.

SCIENTIST 2: Amazing. *(to SCIENTIST 3)* Write this down. Subject 1640 displays independent joy despite lack of new stimuli. Subject may be a genius.

SCIENTIST 1: What?

SCIENTIST 2: Humor is another key to their survival. Considering their history, it's clear her people are...were remarkably resilient.

SCIENTIST 3: *(reading device)* Here it says that the male of their species died out earlier from —

SCIENTIST 1: Like the dinosaur they became extinct!

SCIENTIST 2: No, they began to disappear before the female. Studies show after episodes of repeated and extreme violence —

SCIENTIST 1: I think they were pretty violent —

SCIENTIST 2: — and prolonged disease began to decrease the male population.

SCIENTIST 3: What kind of disease?

SCIENTIST 1: Probably something to do with their large —

SCIENTIST 2: You are really insane. That has never been proven.

SCIENTIST 1: I'm just saying…

SCIENTIST 3: But how did some of the women survive?

> *BLACK WOMAN puts down her pen and opens the suitcase. She takes out a stack of sepia and black and white photographs and slowly places them side by side.*

SCIENTIST 2: Good question.

SCIENTIST 3: I wonder if the subject does different things when we're not observing her.

SCIENTIST 1: Not likely. I don't think she's capable of much range.

SCIENTIST 3: I'd lose my mind if I had to be like her. Alone like that all the time. Every day. Every week. Every year. Nobody to be close to. To touch or —

SCIENTIST 2: She's been alone for a long time. Most of her life, I think. Very little companionship. Isolation.

SCIENTIST 1: That's almost become her natural habitat. It was a gradual shift, but for the last thirty years or so most of them lived under similar conditions. When the men…um, disappeared —

SCIENTIST 2: No friends? No children. That can't be. It just seems so cruel. I guess it's natural selection.

SCIENTIST 1: That's science.

> BLACK WOMAN *takes the makings of the quilt out of the suitcase and beings to make a collage out of the photographs using the quilt to frame the photos.*

SCIENTIST 2: And history.

SCIENTIST 3: What is she making?

SCIENTIST 1: Some kind of quilt. Another old-fashioned art form brought back to haunt us.

SCIENTIST 3: She's good. It's lovely. What do you usually feed her? I mean, what does she eat?

SCIENTIST 2: We generally supply basic meals.

SCIENTIST 1: Yep. But we try to provide cultural dishes on special occasions, but I heard she didn't like the ribs and chitterlings we brought in last month.

SCIENTIST 2: You're gross, you know that? *(to SCIENTIST 3)* Her paperwork says she is a vegan.

SCIENTIST 1: Imagine that.

SCIENTIST 3: Who are they? In the photographs?

SCIENTIST 2: Pictures of her mother and father. Her parents died when she was two.

SCIENTIST 3: Part of the purge, or —

SCIENTIST 1: The war.

SCIENTIST 3: What a suicide mission. They rebelled?

SCIENTIST 2: Our records indicate her parents were part of the final insurrection.

SCIENTIST 3: They never had a chance.

SCIENTIST 2: But they took it anyway.

SCIENTIST 3: Yep. That's quite a story. Pretty amazing to think she's still here.

SCIENTIST 1: Yeah, a descendent of Harriet Tubman, Fannie Lou Hamer, Angela Davis and Oprah.

SCIENTIST 3: Exceptional stock.

SCIENTIST 1: I was kidding.

SCIENTIST 3: Really? Well, it doesn't matter if you were joking or not. Her parents seem pretty outstanding. Will that skew the results?

SCIENTIST 2: Maybe. *(A report comes in on the device.)* Oh my God! They found one. A male of their species.

SCIENTIST 1: What? A black man. Are you serious?

SCIENTIST 2: Yes, it says he was hiding among the people of Quadrant E1954 —Southern Europe. He figured he'd be safe there but he was captured and brought back here.

SCIENTIST 1: What for?

SCIENTIST 2: *(reading)* No. It can't be. This hasn't happened in nearly twenty years.

SCIENTIST 3: *(reading over SCIENTIST 2's shoulder)* Breed them? Wow.

SCIENTIST 2: So they want to make more? To replenish the race?

SCIENTIST 1: Why? And then what?

SCIENTIST 2: I don't know if it will work.

SCIENTIST 3: Is this legal? Can they do that? Where will they live? How will they —

SCIENTIST 2: I don't know. I couldn't possibly imagine.

SCIENTIST 3: The potential impact of this will be monumental.

SCIENTIST 1: *(Timer goes off.)* Finally. Time's up!

> *The SCIENTISTS begin to confirm their observations.*
>
> *While they work, BLACK WOMAN looks up from her quilting and begins to laugh again. This time louder and more robustly. She laughs so hard she begins to cry. First her tears are tears of laughter, but then they become tears of sorrow. Deep, haunting sorrow. The earth begins to shake again and it's not clear whether her grief makes the walls fall or if it's just Mother Nature or both. She is freed. She begins to walk toward the SCIENTISTS. SCIENTIST 1 screams and runs out of the room in terror but SCIENTIST 2 and SCIENTISTS 3 stand frozen partly from a mix of fascination, desire and disgust.*
>
> *Dark*

End of Play

OUT OF INK 2017: Object Lessons

Ingredients:

1. The play must somehow feature the thoughts/statements of an inanimate object.
2. The play must contain a ritual of inauguration.
3. Time continually expands or contracts for at least one of the characters.

The ingredients were contributed by Steven Dietz, Professor of Playwriting and Directing at the University of Texas; Artistic Director of Theatre en Bloc, Jenny Lavery; and Obie Award-winning performance artist/writer/director, Katie Pearl.

The original production was at Hyde Park Theatre, 511 W. 43rd St. in Austin, April 27-29 and May 4-6, 2017 with the following company:

Playwrights: Rita Anderson, Lowell Bartholomee, Trey Deason, Amparo Garcia-Crow, Raul Garza, Max Langert, Jason Rainey, and Sarah Saltwick

Directors: Ellie McBride, Rudy Ramirez, Sharon Sparlin, and Lily Wolff

Performers: Mateo Barrera, Amy Chang, Karina Dominguez, David DuBose, Gina Houston, Michael Joplin, Matrex Kilgore, Gricelda Silva, Reagan Tankersley, Katy Taylor, and Johanna Whitmore

Designers: Lowell Bartholomee (sound), Pam Friday (costumes), Taylor Harrison (sets/props), and Jennifer Rogers (lights)

Production Staff:
Stage Manager: Patti Neff-Tiven
Assistant Stage Manager: Callie Stribling

Light Board Operator: Elizabeth Miller
Sound Operator: Patti Neff-Tiven

ScriptWorks Staff:
Executive Artistic Director: Christina J. Moore
Member Representative: Max Langer

SMILEY
Lowell Bartholomee
© 2017

FOR DIRK

CHARACTERS

SMILEY, *a 16-year-old dog*
THIS ONE, *his owner*
THE OTHER ONE, *his other owner*
CHEWIE, *a chew toy that's seen better days*
DOC, *a veterinarian*

In the dark:

CHEWIE: Smiley.

> *Lights suddenly up. SMILEY in the middle of the stage. He used to be down, but he comes up with the lights, supporting himself on his arms. The rest of his body remains immobile. He looks around quickly.*

SMILEY: I'm awake. Awake! Where is everybody? Where'd they go? Where have they been?!

> *THIS ONE and THE OTHER ONE enter.*

SMILEY: Never mind. Hi. Hi. Hi! Hi! Hi! Hi!

> *As SMILEY does this he tries to push himself up, but only his arms work and everything else is dead weight. It's a struggle and becomes painful.*

SMILEY: Hi! Hi. Hi hi hi hi. Ow.

The humans rush to SMILEY and ease him down, draping themselves on him.

THIS ONE: Good boy good boy good boy good boy.

THE OTHER ONE:
Good good good good GOOD BOY.

Good to note here that we hear their dialogue only as SMILEY hears it. The same words over and over again. In this case, they're really just talking SMILEY down and telling him not to get up. From here on out, intended dialogue will be in parentheses after what we hear.

SMILEY: Sorry. Sorry. I should have nailed that. I'm usually good at standing up. It's a talent of mine. I'm having an off day.

THIS ONE: Good boy good boy. (It's okay, stay down.)

THE OTHER ONE:
LOVE you Smiley.

SMILEY: You left the room days ago and now you're back. You do that all the time.

The doorbell rings. The humans aren't happy to hear it. They get up.

SMILEY: See? You're doing it now, aren't you? I won't see you again for another month, will I?

THIS ONE and THE OTHER ONE look at each other. This is a tough moment.

SMILEY: Ummm. You didn't have to stop petting me.

>*THIS ONE picks up CHEWIE, which has been sitting behind SMILEY this whole time out of his sight line. THIS ONE places it in front of SMILEY.*

THIS ONE: Good boy Chewie good boy good boy.

>*SMILEY locks eyes with CHEWIE.*

THE OTHER ONE:
Smiley… Smiley…

>*THE OTHER ONE almost breaks. THIS ONE leads them out of the room. SMILEY continues to stare at CHEWIE.*

SMILEY: Where did they find you?

CHEWIE: Right where you left me.

SMILEY: I was coming back for you.

CHEWIE: Uh huh.

SMILEY: I was coming to get you today.

CHEWIE: Really.

SMILEY: I was only gone for a second.

CHEWIE: Uh huh.

SMILEY: Point is you're back. Just like old times. Except now it hurts when I chew things and my back end doesn't work so well. But I'm sure that's just temporary.

THIS ONE, THE OTHER ONE, and DOC enter.

SMILEY: You're back! And you brought a stranger! Listen, Stranger! Normally I'd give you a good barking and paw you right in the groin but…

DOC bends to SMILEY and strokes his face.

DOC: You have nothing to feel bad about, you majestic gentleman. You're perfect as you are.

SMILEY is struck dumb by this. Just stares.

DOC: (*to humans*) Let's talk for a bit. No need to hurry this.

DOC gets back up. The humans exit. THE OTHER ONE lingers a bit, not wanting to break contact with SMILEY. Soon all humans are gone.

SMILEY: Did you see that?

CHEWIE: See what?

SMILEY: The Stranger understood me.

CHEWIE: I understand you.

SMILEY: But The Stranger has two legs. And looks a lot better than you do.

CHEWIE: The Stranger hasn't been under a pile of dead leaves since the Bush Administration.

SMILEY: Something is wrong.

CHEWIE: It was a long time to be alone.

SMILEY: No, something is really wrong here. The humans have been weird lately. All they do is cry. For the last year all they do is cry. And now this Stranger appears out of nowhere.

> *SMILEY tries to get up again, ends up turning himself around and around.*

SMILEY: …get to the bottom of this…

> *SMILEY yelps. That last part hurt bad. He falls. His humans and DOC enter.*

THIS ONE: SMILEY. SMILEY. SMILEY. Good boy. (Smiley! Don't get up, just stay down!)

THE OTHER ONE:
(*to DOC*) Smiley dog dog dog dog boy Smiley bad. (This is how it's been. And when we're not here…)

DOC: I think it's time.

SMILEY: It is time. I don't know what you're up to, but I want you to know I'm onto you, Stranger.

THIS ONE: Shhh shhhhhhh shhhhhhhhh.

SMILEY: We used to Go around here. They'd say go and we'd GO. The park with all the lesser dogs. The one with the wicked river that always tried to lure me in, but I always resisted.

THE OTHER ONE:

	Good good boy.
SMILEY:	Now. Now they don't say Go. They just carry me to the car and we go to the white room that smells like all the pee and another Stranger pokes me.
THIS ONE:	Love you good boy.
SMILEY:	Socks go unchewed. I don't get to behair the couch anymore.
THE OTHER ONE:	
	Good boy.
SMILEY:	And now here you are.
DOC:	Let me get things ready.

SMILEY's humans reluctantly leave his side. The humans exit.

SMILEY:	If this keeps up I'll be forced to go negative. I have plenty on both of them and I'm not too proud to name names.
CHEWIE:	Smiley, I know this is a delicate time.
SMILEY:	That One? You can't imagine how many times when they're alone they put on that loud song and dance in their underwear.
CHEWIE:	And the words of an abandoned chew toy may not be helpful.
SMILEY:	Like a lot of times. Like think of all the times you can think of and then add a thousand times.

CHEWIE: But if I've learned anything in my short, uneventful life it's that the ones who love you can be really bad at showing it sometimes.

SMILEY: The Other One? Terrible record of not sharing their ice cream. Terrible!

CHEWIE: And just because you get buried in the backyard doesn't mean you've been forgotten.

DOC enters with their bag.

SMILEY: *(accusing)* You.

DOC: *(admiring)* You.

SMILEY: I hope you have time because there's a lot —

DOC: There's not much time.

SMILEY: Then I'll be brief.

DOC: I need you to listen.

SMILEY: I'm good at that.

DOC: You've probably noticed that those two have been acting strange for about *(calculates)* seven or so of your years, haven't you?

SMILEY: I may have noticed a few things.

DOC: It's been a rough time for the humans. We've lost a lot of our best. A prince, a champ, an exceptional thief, a rebel princess, a starman, and a five-foot assassin. And lots more.

SMILEY: Oh.

DOC: And our worst get more powerful.

SMILEY: They used to wake up and scratch my belly. Now they just look at their little glowing screen and say, "Oh, what the fuck now?!"

DOC: That's why.

SMILEY: When that evil man with the bag comes to the door every day, they need me to bark him away. So, get your best people to come back and bark the bad ones away.

DOC: Maybe they need a leader to show them how.

SMILEY: Then tell that leader to get off their butt and get to work.

DOC: That's… kind of why I'm here.

DOC and SMILEY look at each other a bit.

SMILEY: No, get outta here.

DOC: Only if you choose to accept the position.

SMILEY: Why me?

DOC: Because with everything else, if what's about to happen isn't for the greater good, this moment is too dark to comprehend.

SMILEY: I'd have to leave here.

DOC: Yes. But if you love them…

SMILEY: I do love them. Them and chicken. Not in that order. But I don't want to leave. They won't be able to continue.

DOC: The ones we lost? They're waiting for you. They need you.

SMILEY: Not that they act that way. I think I make them sad. Except when I wet my bed. Then they get irritated.

DOC: They don't mean to be —

SMILEY: They try not to. But I do it a lot now.

DOC: They're under an incredible amount of —

SMILEY: Lately I wet the bed a lot. I can't help it.

DOC: I know. It's —

SMILEY: I don't want to, I just pee —

DOC: We can change the subject.

SMILEY: Sorry, I get fixated on things. You may not have noticed.

DOC: We wouldn't ask you to do this if it weren't important.

SMILEY: Mmmmm. Look, pal, don't cover a pill with cream cheese and call it a treat. I've been here long enough to know a trick when I see it.

CHEWIE: Uh huh.

DOC: Sorry.

SMILEY: Just because I fall for them every single time doesn't mean I don't see right through them.

CHEWIE: Hmm.

DOC: It doesn't mean you aren't special.

SMILEY: You're damn right I'm special. You should worship me.

DOC reveals the syringes.

DOC: I'm afraid this is all I have to offer.

SMILEY studies the syringes for a long moment.

SMILEY: These humans I'm going to lead, I better not get any backtalk.

DOC: I'm sure they'll be respectful.

SMILEY: It'll be what I want, when I want, no questions asked.

DOC: Don't let it go to your head.

SMILEY: I'll be stern but fair. *(pause)* Can you send them back in? They've been out there for months.

DOC: *(giving injections)* Of course. Thank you, boy. Tell them we tried.

DOC finishes up and exits. THIS ONE and THE OTHER ONE enter and drape themselves on SMILEY. They whisper their final messages to him a steady stream of "good dog," "love you." etc. It becomes a hushed underscore to the rest of this.

SMILEY: You didn't do this enough. Come down here like this. You have no idea how lonely it is below knee level. It's worse when you're gone. I know. You have to leave for some reason. Almost every day you had to leave the house and potentially starve me. I'll never understand that. But thank you for coming back every time and bringing the sun back with you.

The lights have gradually gotten brighter. SMILEY pushes himself up on his front legs and looks out.

SMILEY: Has that wall always been a welcoming embrace of pure light and I just never noticed it before? Don't feel bad about… whatever it was I was just talking about. Suddenly it doesn't bother me. I'm glad you're here. I was always glad you were here. Try not to break everything before I come back.

CHEWIE: Goodbye, Smiley.

SMILEY: You're coming with me.

CHEWIE: Ahhhh, shit.

SMILEY: Treat everybody like you now wish you could have treated me every day. You'd be amazed —

Wow!

Just…Be good.

Lights down.

End of Play

OUT OF INK 2018: Lost & Found

Ingredients:

1. An object lost 20 years ago is found.
2. At least one character must experience a reversal of fortune.
3. The play must include a folk dance.

In honor of our 20th Anniversary Season and the 20th Out of Ink, we returned to our original contributors, casting director, Vicky Boone, Arts Editor for the Austin Chronicle, Robert Faires, and playwright Sherry Kramer.

The original production ran April 26-28 and May 3-5, 2018 at Hyde Park Theatre, 511 W. 43rd St. in Austin with the following company:

Playwrights: Robin Anderson, Martha Lynn Coon, Pelita Dasalla, Ava Love Hanna, Max Langert, Sandy Maranto, Briandaniel Oglesby, and Megan Thornton.

Directors: Ellie McBride, Christina J. Moore, Rudy Ramirez, and Sharon Sparlin

Performers: David Barrera, Roxy Becker, Karina Dominguez, David DuBose, Matrex Kilgore, Cherry Mendoza, Mindy Rast-Keenan, Taji Senior, Nguyen Stanton, Rommel Sulit, and Vincent Tomasino

Designers: Lowell Bartholomee (sound and video), Pam Friday (costumes), Amy Lewis (lights), and Patti Neff-Tiven (sets/props)

Production Staff:

Stage Manager: Patti Neff-Tiven
Asst. Stage Manager: Kelsey Moringy

Sound/Video Operator: Patti Neff-Tiven

ScriptWorks Staff:
Executive Artistic Director: Christina J. Moore
Member Representative: Max Langert

BIG BRAD WOLF
Ava Love Hanna
© 2017

CHARACTERS
WOLF, *calm, deep and new-agey, struggling to break free of old patterns.*
PIG, *energetic, whimsical, pushy*
RED, *bossy, abrasive, intimidating*
JOEY, *clueless, speaks with a thick New Jersey accent.*

SCENE
In the front yard of a small cabin, deep in the enchanted woods.

WOLF is sitting in full lotus position meditating and chanting lightly. PIG enters, sees WOLF and excitedly runs over to where he is sitting.

WOLF: *(meditating)* Oooooooom. *(breathes deeply)* Ooooooooom.

PIG circles WOLF watching curiously for a moment. He then starts poking him in the shoulder.

WOLF: Ooooooom. Ooooooomy God, what are you doing?!

PIG: I'm poking you in the shoulder. What are YOU doing?

WOLF: I'm meditating. I'm finding my center so I can face the day. I'm looking for the middle path.

PIG: *(not impressed)* Well, that's weird. So, where the hell have you been? The only path you need to find is the one to my house.

WOLF: I was on sabbatical. I needed to get away from here to figure some things out. Clear my head.

PIG: Well, you stood me up. So, there I was sitting in a straw house waiting for it to be blown down and you never showed up! I sat there for 2 weeks.

WOLF: Why didn't you leave and do something else?

PIG: *(indignant)* Do something else?? Like what? My plans for the day were: sit in straw house, get eaten by Big Bad Wolf.

WOLF: Don't call me that.

PIG: What?

WOLF: Big BAD Wolf. It's not my name. My name is Brad.

PIG: Soooo, you want me to call you the Big Brad Wolf?? So, when you come running after us to eat us, we're all supposed to scream "Run, run, it's the Big Brad Wolf!"

WOLF: Well, it is my name.

PIG: *(disgusted)* I don't like it; I'm not gonna do it.

WOLF: And, you don't need to run from me. I'm not doing that stuff anymore.

PIG: WHAT?!

WOLF: I no longer eat pigs.

PIG: Dude, it's your job! Your job is to be big and scary and to eat pigs.

WOLF: No, it's not.

PIG: Uh, yes it is. It's what Big Bad, er, "Brad" Wolves do.

WOLF: No, I was just perpetuating an unhealthy cycle taught to me by my dysfunctional parents.

PIG: *(rolls eyes)* What are you eating then? Cows? Chickens? Gnomes?

WOLF: Well, I've been eating a lot of tofu. I found this fake bacon that's really —

PIG: *(interrupts him)* Ewww. No. Just no. No one likes tofu. Wow, you really do hate yourself.

WOLF: Do you think I wanted to eat pigs? Like, I just woke up one day and was like mmm eating pigs sounds delicious!

PIG: We are delicious.

WOLF: No, you taste like paternal guilt, like fear of change.

PIG: No, I'm pretty sure I taste rich and smoky with just a hint of applewood.

WOLF: *(shudders)* You taste like failure.

PIG: What?!

RED enters.

RED: *(to WOLF)* Hey, Big Bad Loser! Where the hell have you been? My Grandmother should be working her way through your lower intestine by now.

PIG: Uh, he goes by Brad now, so that would be Big Brad Loser.

RED: Shut up, pork rind. Shouldn't you be on a spit somewhere?

PIG: Exactly! That's what I've been trying to tell him! He doesn't want to eat me and it's really disappointing.

RED: Look here Wolf, I am tired of wasting away in this forest. Do you know how hard it is to meet anyone out here? I'm constantly delivering baked goods to this old lady. She's on her 6th pie this week! Your job is to eat my grandmother, so that a handsome, burly woodsman with an axe can come rescue me.

WOLF: That's not who I am. I don't want to hurt old ladies. And wait a minute, wouldn't that result in me being killed by the woodsman?

RED: Collateral damage. I'm not getting any younger and this hood isn't getting any looser. I want to find my soul mate and instead I'm out here running a geriatric baked goods delivery service.

PIG: You know, he eats tofu now.

RED: Gross. Also, I don't care. Now, stop doing whatever weird stuff you guys are doing over here and go eat my grandmother so I can get

	rescued. I'm tired of "delivering my own cookies," IF you know what I mean.
WOLF:	No.
RED:	Oh, you know what I mean.
WOLF:	Yes, I know. I'm saying no because it's awful and I don't want to think about it.
RED:	Stop being a baby and start eating pigs and old ladies. Start with this guy, he is the worst. *(points at PIG)*.
PIG:	Yes! Eat me!
WOLF:	You know what, you guys are dicks. Most friends want their friends to be happy, to be better people. You just want me to be a gluttonous murderer with high cholesterol.
RED:	I want you to do your job. If you don't eat my grandmother, who will?
PIG:	And have you been to pig village lately? We are eyeball deep in piglets. We have 12 babies at a time, twice a year. I have 300 nieces and nephews. You need to eat me before Christmas because I just don't have the cash for that.
	PIG proceeds to sit down in a chair, bastes himself in butter, and opens a sun-tanning reflector.
WOLF:	It doesn't have to be this way. You guys are acting like you're living in a pre-written story. There are so many possibilities.

RED: Whatever. I've got more cookies to deliver. *(Gets in the WOLF's face)* Take care of the old woman.

RED exits.

PIG: Eww, which kind of cookies do you think she meant? I didn't see a basket…

WOLF: What are you doing?

PIG: Basting myself. It will make my skin crispy and delicious for you.

WOLF: *(sigh)* I used to get up and terrorize pigs every day because it's all I knew. I did it because my father did it, and his father before him and his father before him. It was the only thing we had in common, the only thing to talk about. My dad didn't care about anything else. Did you know that he was so obsessed with pigs that he called Monday, Pig Day? He also called Tuesday, Pig Day. He called every day of the week Pig Day. Do you know how confusing that was? He'd say "Pick me up from work on Pig Day." I never knew when to be there!

PIG: He sounds like a great guy — a guy who knew how to do his job. Oh, speaking of your dad, while you were gone I found something in your house that belonged to him.

WOLF: You went in my house?

PIG: Yeah, well, you weren't here, so I let myself in and started rooting around. I found this book hidden under a floor board.

PIG reaches into backpack and pulls out a small, dusty journal and hands it to WOLF.

WOLF: Wait, this is my dad's journal! I've been looking for this for 20 years. I bet he felt the same as me. I bet he hid this because he didn't want anyone to know that he was also struggling with this life.

PIG: Um, maybe. Let's read it.

WOLF opens book and begins to read aloud.

WOLF: Pig Day: Ate Pig. *(turns page)* Pig Day: Ate 5 Pig. *(flips ahead a few more pages)* Pig Day: Ate 2 Pig today. I love eating pig. I feel so fulfilled with this life and need nothing more.

PIG: What a great guy. Oh look! There's recipes in the back. *(points to page)* Hey! That's how my buddy from college went out. He was on vacation in Hawaii.

WOLF: *(sighs heavily)* Well, this sucks. And, his arteries must have been so clogged. I don't want to eat pigs! I want to connect with pigs. I want to feel the heart connection between all living things. *(WOLF turns to face PIG.)*

Little Pig, Little Pig, let me come in. *(WOLF places his hand on PIG's heart.)*

PIG: *(jumps back)* Eww, don't touch me unless you are eating me.

JOEY THE PIG enters.

JOEY: Yo, Little, did you do the thing? Did you get him to eat you, yet?

PIG: *(rolls eyes and sighs)* Joey, come here for a minute. Look, at me. I want you to really look at me for a minute, do I look like I've been eaten by a wolf?

JOEY: *(Stands and stares at PIG for a while. Looks him over.)* Uh, no?

PIG: That's right, no. I have not been eaten by the wolf. *(to WOLF)* Do you see what I'm dealing with every day over there? You want to make the world a better place? Eat us by the handful. *(to JOEY)* Hey Joey, while you're here, help me out with something. We need to do our dance for him.

JOEY: Which dance? The Dab?

PIG: No, never that. OUR pig dance, the dance of our people. La Chicharrón.

JOEY: Oh, right. *(JOEY pulls a tiny maraca out of his backpack and shakes it rhythmically.)*

PIG: *(Begins singing to the tune of La Cucaracha)*
We're made of bacon *(rubs belly)*
And also pork chops *(points to shoulder)*
And I'm made of some ham too *(turns around and shakes butt)*
You should eat us, we are delicious *(spins back around)*
You can put us in a stew!

WOLF: Just stop it! I'm not eating anyone today.

PIG: Well, thanks, Joey, looks like I'll be here a bit longer.

JOEY: Okay, I'm gonna head out. I've got a shift at the stick factory. Those flimsy houses ain't gonna build themselves.

JOEY exits.

PIG: So, this is it, huh? You're just gonna stop being bad?

WOLF: Yes. I just want a chance to live my life my way. See what I like and dislike, explore the world, figure out who I am. You could do that too, you know.

PIG: Me? I could? I mean, I always assumed I would be eaten by now. I never really planned to have a future. But, you know, now that you've mentioned it, I've always wanted to go to Disney World.

WOLF: You can do that! Heck, I'll go with you.

PIG: But, what about everyone else? What will happen here?

WOLF: They'll be fine. They'll figure it out. Everyone deserves a chance to find their own path, to write their own story.

RED enters.

RED: Alright, losers. I knew I couldn't count on you, so I did your job for you.

PIG: *(shocked)* You ate your grandmother?!

RED: No, idiot. I dumped her in a retirement home like any good granddaughter.

PIG: Well, then how are you going to meet someone?

RED: I signed up for one of those online dating apps.

WOLF: Tinder?

RED: No dummy, I'm not into fire fighters. I want a woodsman, so I signed up for the axe related one, Grindr.

PIG: uh…

RED: So, it seems like my luck has changed. I signed up as "Big Red" and mentioned I was into axe play and before I could even put up a profile pic, I got pinged by a real buff looking guy named BigBear69. He seems perfect. I'm about to meet him in the park. I bet we get married this week. So, bye idiots. My new life awaits!

RED exits.

PIG: Oh my god, we HAVE to tell her. *(Starts to walk off, WOLF stops him.)*

WOLF: No, no we don't.

PIG: Wait… you're still bad aren't you?

WOLF: Maybe just a little. Want to come inside for a kombucha?

PIG: Sure, why not.

WOLF and PIG exit together.

End of Play

www.ingramcontent.com/pod-product-compliance
Lightning Source LLC
Chambersburg PA
CBHW071155070526
44584CB00019B/2805